Keep Moving On

The Migration of a Punjabi-Sikh Family

Amrit Singh

To my parents—thank you for everything.

To Alina, Millin, and Hazel—the world is yours.

Glossary of Family Relations

Dhadhi Ji	Paternal grandmother
Dhadha Ji	Paternal grandfather
Nani Ji	Maternal grandmother
Nana Ji	Maternal grandfather
Thaya Ji	Father's older brother
Thayi Ji	Thaya's wife; father's sister-in-law
Chacha Ji	Father's younger brother
Chachi Ji	Chacha's wife; father's sister-in-law
Bhua Ji	Father's sister
Fufar Ji	Bhua's husband; father's brother-in-law
Massi Ji	Mother's sister
Massar Ji	Massi's husband; mother's brother-in-law
Mamma Ji	Mother's brother
Mammi Ji	Mamma's wife; mother's sister-in-law
Auntie	Older female relative or family friend
Uncle	Older male relative or family friend

This book is accompanied by a soundtrack performed by the author, and features production and guest appearances from EMPWER, Daysdeaf, Selena Dhillon, Keerat Kaur, B Magic, Jasmin Kaur, and Vaz.

To download/stream the soundtrack, scan the image below.

Table of Contents

CHAPTER
(ONE)
PRESERVATION

In the song "A Story No One Told," rapper Shad tells the tale of a man who is visited by death. In his final moments, the man witnesses his life flash before his eyes. He relives memories of the love he shared with his wife, small and forgotten moments from his youth, places around his hometown that he had visited, and seeing his children grow. Recognizing that his life is ending, the man asks for an opportunity to write his story with a piece of chalk on the city streets. Time stands still and allows for the man to cover the concrete with his writings. When the man completes his final act and passes away, his neighbours are moved to tears upon discovering the story he had left behind for them. The man wasn't famous or rich, but his life still mattered and carried beauty and meaning in its details. The song posits that the greatest stories are those of ordinary people living ordinary lives.

Under the shadow of the CN tower, there are similar stories. Not of wealth or glory, but of ordinary people who have come from afar and still carry the soils of home on the bottoms of their feet. These are regular people with families, friends, dreams, and fears—the same as all of us—but their definitions of ordinary have been coloured by social, economic, and political factors outside of their control. Usually it's the ordinary people who are hurt the most by these variables.

African American writer and activist James Baldwin said that history does not exist in the past, but in the present; we carry our history with us. The Punjabi man in Brampton with grease under his fingernails who uses his hands to repair truck engines had to outrun German Shepherds to flee from immigration officials in Europe decades ago. The Jamaican schoolteacher in Toronto had spent his youth in England being harassed by extremist groups who believed that a racially integrated nation was an affront to white supremacy and purity. The nurse at the methadone clinic in Mississauga was born to parents who travelled north on foot to find safety away from the civil war in El Salvador. The mental health counsellor in Scarborough is a miracle baby who was carried by a mother who had suffered gunshot wounds while pregnant during the genocide in Sri Lanka. Though all of these people arrived in Canada under uncertainty and confusion, they all shared the collective hope that their roots would grow in new ground and reform within the fertility of that darkness.

Growing up and living in the Greater Toronto Area, a part of the world known for its diversity and multiculturalism, I've crossed paths with all of the people mentioned above. Some of them I'm lucky enough to call colleagues, friends, and family. We all have stories of where we're from and why we couldn't stay there, and in a global landscape shaped by colonialism and displacement, we all have different paths of how we got here, as well as an understanding of what it means not to be from here.

This writing is my attempt at uncovering the lives of the ordinary people closest to me, namely my father. As ordinary people, we often feel that our lives are not worth documenting, that our experiences aren't special enough to merit preservation. However, as generations age and elders pass on, our ability to tell our own stories is lost. In writing this book, I wanted to give my father's story a degree of permanence that we tend not to reserve for ordinary people. My hope is that in reading about his life—the love he shared with his wife, the small and forgotten memories of his youth, the places around the world that he visited in his migration, and seeing his children grow—you will see that all people are capable of courage, strength, and a resilience to keep moving on.

CHAPTER
DEATH IS CERTAIN
TWO

A team of twelve loaded the casket into the back of the black hearse. Over the low hum of prayer and the sobs of onlookers, the shuffles of footsteps belonging to the sons and relatives of Gurmukh Singh Sohal carried his body to its final destination of Markeaton Crematorium in Derby, England. White floral arrangements on the side of the spotless Cadillac spelled out the many titles he held: Dad. Husband. Boss. Mr. Sohal.

My father Satnam Singh was one of the twelve that carried Gurmukh's casket. He and Gurmukh were cousins. I referred to Gurmukh as Thaya Ji—my father's older brother. He and Dad were just a year apart in age. Dad stood on the lawn outside of the crematorium, surrounded by his and Thaya Ji's family and friends who all held gold and navy blue balloons. At the conclusion of the funeral proceedings, they released the balloons in unison and watched them dance in the wind, first against the forest green of the trees that lined the crematorium grounds, and then against the ashen grey of the overcast clouds.

In 1966, Gurmukh Thaya Ji had moved from his village of Sangal Sohal in the northern Indian state of Punjab to the United Kingdom when he was thirteen years old. He was joined by his brothers Makhan and Charanjit, his mother Chanan Kaur, and his father Nazar Singh. Back when India was still a British colony, Nazar had served in the army during World War II as part of the fire brigade. In 1963, Nazar was granted a job voucher in India that allowed him to apply for a position with the fire department in Wolverhampton in the UK. Drawn by the allure of higher earning potential in the West, Nazar's arrival in England didn't play out the way he had envisioned. He was told during the job interview with the fire department in Wolverhampton that he didn't speak English well enough to join their ranks. Now in a new country and denied the job that was the catalyst for why he had left home in the first place, Nazar moved from Wolverhampton to Derby and rented a house with a handful of other Punjabi immigrants. They found work together as labourers at a local metal foundry, which was a physically demanding job that Nazar considered to be a demotion from his ranking with the military. He didn't let his bitterness sway him from his goal though, and he saved up as much money as he could with each paycheque. By 1966, Nazar returned to his village of Sangal Sohal to gather his wife and three sons, and they moved to England to begin their new lives together.

Growing up in Derby as a teenager in the late sixties, Gurmukh secured his first full-time job as a labourer on a construction site. In the seventies, he found employment with British Rail as a train conductor. Around the same time, he also began packing and selling Indian spices out of his garage to restaurant owners in Derby and neighbouring cities in the midlands area. His side hustle blossomed and he left the rails behind to start his own business, Sohal Food Store, which became one of the first shops in the region to specialize in South Asian foods and spices. He shared his success with others and dedicated portions of his earnings towards the construction of roads, streetlights, and the modernization of the sewage and drainage infrastructure in Sangal Sohal.

I didn't learn any of these stories of Thaya Ji's life from him or from my father. Dad didn't talk much about where he came from or where he'd been before our family settled outside of Punjab. No one from the older generations in my family did. I pieced Thaya Ji's story together on my own from articles published online by local media outlets in Derby in the aftermath of his passing. Part of what drove my research was that I felt like I didn't know Thaya Ji well enough to mourn him. He regularly made long-distance phone calls from the UK to our house in Canada to speak with Dad about Gurbani, family, and health, and I saw Thaya Ji every few years when one of us made the trip across the pond to visit, but aside from the fact that he was my uncle, I still felt like I didn't know much about who he was as a person—what drove him, what his life was like growing up, and what events and experiences shaped him.

One article I found after Thaya Ji died showed a photo of him from what looked to be the late eighties or early nineties. In the picture, he sat at a desk in a cramped office wearing a white golf shirt, powder blue dastaar, and a smile on his bearded face. On a shelf above him were binders, letter trays, and banker's boxes. On the door behind him was a painting of Guru Gobind Singh Ji. In the article, former business partners spoke highly of who Thaya Ji was, how he helped their business ventures grow, the money and time he had invested towards local causes in Derby, and the legacy he left behind. He was a giant in his community and I didn't even know it.

***

In April 2017, just a few months before Gurmukh Thaya Ji died, I lost my Mom's mom—my Nani Ji, Pritam Kaur—to a heart attack.

I had lived with both sets of grandparents at different points of my life. Dad always said it was his duty to look after the elders as they aged the same way they had looked after him when he was growing up. My grandparents were an integral part of our household when I was young, providing guidance and supervision when my parents worked jobs at varying hours throughout the day. Dad had his consistent work schedule and routine: he typically woke up at 3:00 a.m. to meditate before he left home at 6:00 a.m. for his job in North York where he manufactured furniture. He would return twelve or thirteen hours later, and his time at home in the evenings was mostly spent in solitude. My conversations with him didn't expand much past the usual pleasantries. How was work? Fine. How was school? Fine. Dad would wash up, find a quiet place to recite his evening prayers, eat dinner, and go to bed early so he could to do it all over again the next day.

Mom's schedule wasn't as rigid. She worked for low wages in precarious roles, often bouncing between different factories—usually assembly line or meat packing—and she was shifted from early mornings to graveyard to afternoons every few months. When Mom's schedule changed, Nani Ji was one of the constants during those times. Both Nani Ji and Nana Ji lived with Amarjit Mamma Ji and Sewa Mammi Ji, and their house was just a five-minute walk from the elementary school I attended with my sister Vijay and my cousins Manroop and Savraj. Mamma Ji and Mammi Ji's home became a hub of activity for us kids to hang out after school while we waited for our parents to return from work. Nani Ji always had fruit, cheese sandwiches, hot dogs, or chicken nuggets ready for us before we got in the door at the end of each school day. She'd watch silently and with a smile as the four of us discovered new levels and secrets in *Super Mario World*. Although Nani Ji didn't speak English and likely didn't share our excitement in finally making it out of the Forest of Illusion, nothing warmed her heart and made her face glow more than being in the presence of family.

In the week between Nani's death and her scheduled funeral, the scene at Mamma Ji and Mammi Ji's house played out the same way every day. Punjabi funerals are lengthy affairs; we share in them together and grieve with each other as a community. Guests would arrive shortly after eight in the morning to offer condolences and share their favourite memories of my grandmother. Some combination of me, Vijay, Manroop, Savraj, and my wife Nuvi would serve the guests with tea, snacks, and roti. The guests would stay for an hour or so and leave just after the next visitors arrived. This cycle continued all day long and the last guests wouldn't leave until close to midnight. I didn't recognize who most of the visitors were but everyone's stories were similar: they talked about how loving Nani was, how quiet she was but also how funny she could be, and how much she gave. "She used her heart so much that it was bound to give out at some point," one of the visitors had said. Amarjit Mamma Ji and Sewa Mammi Ji retold the story of how Nani died to every guest that came over. They both looked exhausted by the end of the day, their pink-rimmed eyes rubbed raw from wiping away tears. I wondered if it would serve them better to have time to grieve in private but they didn't break custom.

One evening, over the course of the pre-funeral condolences, I slipped away from the crowd to Mamma Ji's study room and closed the door behind me. I needed some space for myself, to breathe. The blinds were still open and it was dark out. A few days prior, Vijay, Manroop, Savraj, and I had been tasked by our parents with putting together a slideshow of Nani Ji's pictures to be shown at her funeral. The four of us had sat on the floor in this room together and passed photographs back and forth. We laughed at the styles of old clothes our parents used to wear, and how our elders looked when they were younger and still had black hair. Our laughter was bittersweet, tears of both sadness and joy stinging our eyes. I was back in this room alone now. The photographs we had set aside for the slideshow were still where we had left them, stacked on a desk to the left of the window. The rest of the pictures were contained in a grey, opaque plastic bag that sat on a bookshelf across from the desk. I took a seat on the white carpet, loosened the twine drawstring atop the bag and tilted it over. Hundreds of pictures poured out and old memories returned to life like a flashback.

I grabbed a handful of photos. One looked like it was from the mid-nineties. In the picture, Nani and Nana were sitting with my parents on a sofa at the furniture factory that Mamma Ji and Mammi Ji owned in Malton. As I looked at the picture, I could almost smell the sawdust of the furniture frames and hear the buzzing of the electricity flowing through the factory's light panels overhead. I could hear the *bap-bap-bap* of Mamma Ji's staple gun and the grind of the foot pedal on Mammi Ji's sewing machine. I flipped through a few more images, set them aside, and gathered another stack from the pile. I found a picture of Nani Ji sitting with Savraj and me. I looked like I was about four years old. We were in the backyard of Amarjit Mamma Ji's old house on the same narrow patch of grass where we played baseball with plastic bats and tried not to hit balls into the vegetable garden. Nani was wearing a brown shawl over her head and shoulders, and Savraj was sitting in her lap. In the photo, I sat beside Nani and rested my head against her arm. I closed my eyes and tried to transport myself into the moment frozen in the picture. I could feel the comforting embrace of the sun and the dewy cool of the grass beneath us. I felt like I was there with Nani Ji again. I opened my eyes and set that picture aside for myself to take home. I didn't want to lose that memory, to tie it back in the bag and suffocate it again.

The next day, Nani Ji's younger brother, who I'd never met before, arrived from Vancouver to attend the funeral. He shared many of the same characteristics Nani had, most notably his smile had the same softness hers did, and in a way that I could only feel but not describe, being around him felt like being at home. In our conversations, we filled each other in on the details of Nani's life, both he and I making up for lost time. I shared stories with him of how Nani Ji was an important mother figure in my life, and explained the downturn in her health, both physically and mentally, in recent years. He informed me of another brother they had that died during the violence that followed India's partition in 1947. The details of Nani we shared varied in intensity and significance, from the traumatic to the mundane, but they all helped paint a broader picture of a life lived.

Through my talks with Nani Ji's brother, I realized that despite all the years I had shared with my grandmother, I didn't know much about her. I didn't know the names of her parents or the village in Punjab where she grew up. I didn't know she had brothers. It wasn't until well after her passing that I learned she had a baby boy named Surjit who died within a week of being born, and that his death had sent Nani Ji into a deep depression.

It wasn't just Nani Ji's or Gurmukh Thaya Ji's deaths that made me feel like I didn't know much about who these important figures in my life were—I felt that way about many people from the older generations in my family. I knew enough about them to spell out their titles in the floral arrangements I could place in their hearses, but I wanted to know who they were beyond that. We lacked communication between generations—about who we were, where we came from, and how we got here to this point with histories and identities scattered across geographies. I wanted to change that. I felt the story of our family lineage was being eroded by time and death. The pictures and the people that still remained were my best chances at getting to know my elders while they were still alive to tell their own stories, before it was too late.

***

As a child, my father sometimes told me of the places he had travelled to before he and Mom settled in Canada and started a family. He shared anecdotes and experiences like scattered breadcrumbs that stretched across the globe—Sri Lanka, Sweden, Italy, Nigeria, Iran, Argentina, Japan, and many others. I tried to follow the trail of clues but felt lost. He chose not to dive into that time of his life too deeply and spoke of those experiences like they belonged to a past-life of his that he only partially remembered. I knew that he had worked in Greece on a cargo ship in his twenties and that he travelled to all of those countries by sea, but I didn't know how long he worked for. He didn't tell me how or why he got involved in that industry, and how the waters took him from the landlocked region of Punjab to Toronto where my sister and I were born.

After Nani Ji and Gurmukh Thaya Ji had both died just a few months apart, I told Dad that I wanted to learn about his life. He said it was a waste of time; Dad saw his past as something he had to get through to make it to where he is now, but he felt the past had nothing new to offer him.

As the summer of 2017 approached its end, the prospect of death visited us a lot closer to home. I felt I was going to lose another person, and that all of their stories, memories, and experiences would soon be gone with them forever.

***

"Please wait here for a moment," the nurse said. "I'll be right back." She turned on her heel and disappeard down a hallway.

Mom and I always felt out of place in the oncology ward at Sunnybrook Hospital. Everyone else who sat in the waiting room's gray, leather chairs had their heads wrapped in floral-patterned bandanas to hide their hair loss from the radiation treatment. Mom didn't even have cancer. Our presence here felt like we were eavesdropping on the most intimate and harrowing secrets of other people's lives. In the years Mom had been cared for at Sunnybrook in Toronto, her primary doctor changed every few months; what didn't change though were her meetings with Dr. Higgins and the team in the oncology department once every quarter. However, after five years of this routine and still no signs of cancer, this whole process started to feel tedious.

The nurse poked her head through the doorway. "Dr. Higgins will see you now," she said with a wave.

Mom and I rose from our seats to follow. Five steps and a right turn, eight steps and a left. We had walked this path from the waiting room to Dr. Higgins' office so many times that we could do it blindfoled. Inside, Mom and I sat in black, plastic chairs with our backs to the wall. We faced the door and awaited the doctor's arrival.

"Do you want some water?" I asked Mom.

"No, not right now," she responded. I set the water bottle down on the floor. Mom straightened her posture when the doctor walked in.

"It's good to see you again," Dr. Higgins began. "How are you doing today?" He took a seat in a stool directly across from us.

"Not too bad," Mom replied. That was always her go-to answer. Not good, always in some level of discomfort, but not *too* bad.

"I wanted to talk to you about your latest bloodwork results," Dr. Higgins said. He paused to remove his thick, silver-framed glasses and placed them atop his sandy-blond head. He rested his elbows on his knees and leaned in closer. "The reason we kept bringing you back all these years was because we were always concerned that the pain you had been feeling was cancer. This looks like it might be it."

My role in Mom's doctor's appointments had historically been to serve as translator. She didn't always understand medical terminology and she sometimes lost the meaning of what people were saying when they spoke English too quickly. She knew the common words and phrases: ultrasound, blood test, MRI. She'd look over to me when a doctor used words that she wasn't familiar with—shingles, biopsy, laparoscopic— and I'd do my best to explain it back to her in Punjabi. Hearing the news from a familiar face, whether it was me or Dad, helped blunt the edges of some of the diagnoses Mom had received in the past. This time though, Mom didn't turn to me for clarification; she seemed to understand Dr. Higgins loud and clear.

"It's okay though," the doctor continued. "We're going to do whatever we can to work with you and ensure you get the best care possible. You're in good hands here. You've got to think positive." Mom nodded to the rhythm of Dr. Higgins' speech. "We're going to bring you back in a week to run a few more tests," he advised, "so before you leave, just stop at the front desk and they'll give you the details for your next appointment."

A week? She's sick now, I thought. Why was he going to wait another week?

"Do you have any questions?" Dr. Higgins asked.

"No," Mom replied. She finally looked over to me. I shook my head to indicate I had nothing further to ask; I didn't know what else to say.

"Okay, so we'll see you next week," Dr. Higgins said.

He rose from his stool and shook Mom's hand. I picked Mom's water bottle up off the floor and tried to leave the room but stopped myself in the doorway; I couldn't remember whether I was supposed to go right or left to get back to the waiting room.

Mom placed a hand on my shoulder. "This way," she said.

Mom and I didn't say a word to each other on the drive home from the hospital. The banter between the hosts and callers on the Punjabi radio show was the only thing that broke the silence between us. Think positive. I kept repeating Dr. Higgins' words in my head until the sounds lost meaning. I wondered what Mom was thinking but didn't know how to ask her. I tried to read her facial expressions and body language out of the corner of my eye when I looked over my shoulder to check my blindspots, but nothing seemed to be out of the ordinary. As much as I desired more communication with my parents, in that moment, it felt safer to retreat back into the silence that we were accustomed to.

PAST
IS
PRESENT
CH——03

Dr. Higgins met with my parents on August 22, 2017 to run a few additional tests. The assessments confirmed that Mom did indeed have cancer. She was diagnosed with stage two squamous cell carcinoma localized on the left side of her neck. The doctors told us it was only a small growth and that they had caught it early enough to consider this a low-risk operation. Mom's surgery was scheduled for September 13. Relatives and family friends came over to the house every day after learning of Mom's illness. Some of them wore grieving and worried expressions as if Mom was already gone. We served food to everyone who came, regardless of the time of day. It felt the same as it did after Nani Ji died.

Before Mom was diagnosed, I was scheduled to attend an orientation and team-building retreat at a cottage in Blue Mountain from August 25 to 27 as part of a new job I was starting in September with Unity Charity, a non-profit organization that provided arts-based programming to youth in and around Toronto. I didn't want to go but Mom told me that staying home and stressing out wasn't going to change anything. Go enjoy, she said; the cancer would still be here when I got back. I didn't want to leave her side but I knew she was right. Maybe the distraction would help me get my mind off things.

On my first night away, there was news that a meteor shower would be visible from where our cottage was, far from the larger cities and suburbs my new coworkers and I had all travelled in from. A group of ten of us waited until nightfall and walked from our cottage to a nearby beach that didn't have any lights. It was so dark out that we couldn't see when we transitioned from pavement to grass to sand until we felt the firmness of the earth beneath us shift and give way. The moonlight illuminated a sign that warned us that nobody was permitted to be on the beach this late in the night, but we ignored it.

The waters sounded active, rushing and bending in response to the full moon. The moon looked low enough to the earth that I could snatch it from the sky; the reflection of its concrete texture appeared blood red in the waters. My colleagues and I stumbled around the beach in the dark. Some people tripped over inclines in the sand's surface and laughed as they fell, while others sat down on the ground just out of reach from where the tide met land. I laid down on a picnic table and looked up at the sky. A blanket of stars hung low overhead. The space between each twinkling speck was darker than I had ever seen back home, dark enough to hide myself in and not be found. A thin streak of light scratched the sky, quick as a blink, then it disappeared. Nobody around me said anything. I wasn't sure if they saw it. I didn't move from my spot on the table. The hood of my sweatshirt was pulled up behind my head, my hands were folded on my stomach, and my feet dangled over the edge. Another flash appeared in the sky, this one just as brief as the first. I couldn't make out what the people around me were saying but it sounded like they saw that one.

I kept my eyes fixated on the sky and scanned the darkness for more shooting stars. I caught another streak of light in my peripheral sight. I listened to the waves converse with the shore. The sky, stars, and waters were ancient, mysterious, undying. I looked towards the moon and could only think of Mom.

Headlights beamed from the parking lot towards the beach and occluded the stars from view. Sand swirled inside the pathways that the headlights carved out of the dark. The car belonged to someone from the local neighbourhood watch who was enforcing the rule that no one was to be on the beach after hours. I got up from the table into a seated position and brushed the sand from my legs. My coworkers and I began walking back to our cottage in silence. I trailed behind the rest of the group. I wished that I was back home.

***

Hospital visits have been a regular part of my life since I was a kid. I got used to the smells of latex gloves and the alcohol in the hand sanitizer. I could parse meaning from the muffled voices calling out names and colour codes over the intercom. Growing up, it felt like Dad and I visited a relative in hospital every few months. The earliest time that I could remember was when I was about six years old. One of Mom's cousins had been shot in Toronto while driving his cab. He dropped a passenger off at the requested destination, but when it came time to collect the fare, the passenger pulled out a gun. A bullet struck my uncle in the jaw and he was in the hospital for a few weeks. I remember seeing him laid up at Etobicoke General with spots of dried blood leaking through the dressing tied around his head and over his beard like an old-timey toothache remedy. The person who I visited most often in hospital though was my mother.

In the summer of 1998 when I was eleven years old, my parents, my sister Vijay, and I moved from Malton to Brampton. My parents had owned a home in the mid-eighties for a few years before I was born, but for my entire life up until '98, we had only ever lived with other family members. In the late eighties into the early nineties, we lived with Amarjit Mamma Ji, Sewa Mammi Ji, Nana Ji, Nani Ji, and my cousins Manroop and Savraj in Malton. From there, Mom, Dad, Vijay, and I moved to the next block over where we were joined by Dad's parents, Sardara Chacha Ji, Sukhi Chachi Ji, and their daughter Simrat. In 1998, Dad seemed to be the only one excited about the move to Brampton, and he tried to sell me on all the positives our new home would have: it was fully detached, had four bedrooms, and a walkout basement that backed out on to a ravine full of trees and a bike path. Our house in Malton didn't have any of those things. I didn't care though; for all the added amenities we gained, I didn't want us to live on our own and be separated from the rest of the family.

Shortly after we had moved to Brampton, Mom became ill and was taken to hospital. I didn't know the details of what was wrong or how sick she was. None of the adults told Vijay or me very much; all we knew was that Mom's kidneys were in bad shape. Our newer and larger house now felt cavernous and empty. Dad told me and Vijay that it was important for us to pray more.

In our first few months of living in Brampton, the routine was for Dad to come home from work around 5:30 p.m., pick me and Vijay up from the house, and take us to see Mom at the hospital. The seasons were changing from autumn to winter and the sun was sinking in the sky earlier each day. It was always dark by the time Dad picked us up, and even darker by the time we got to see Mom.

"How's school?" Mom whispered. Under the yellow light of the pink metal table lamp next to her hospital bed, I almost didn't recognize her. Mom's face looked heavier, almost swollen, and her cheeks sagged. Dark bags circled her eyes.

"It's fine," I said. I pursed my lips.

I hated my new school. I didn't want to tell Mom how I actually felt though. In the state she was in, I didn't want her to waste energy worrying about me. I didn't want her to know I was having a hard time making new friends, that I was being bullied for wearing a patka, and that I faked a stomach ache on the second day of school to get out of going to class. If Mom was home, she would have seen right through my façade and marched me out the door with my brown paper lunch bag in hand. Between work and spending time at the hospital, Dad didn't have time to check on me the same way Mom would have.

"That's good," Mom said. She lifted her chin and nodded slightly in approval. She blinked slowly. The powder blue blanket that covered her body from her feet to her ribs barely moved with each breath she took.

Vijay sat on the other side of the bed and dipped Mom's limp fingers into a white Styrofoam cup filled with warm water, softening her fingernails enough to trim them with a nail cutter. Dad entered the room and dragged an extra chair behind him. He closed the door and placed the chair next to me.

"Let's pray," he said. He sat down, closed his eyes, and folded his hands in his lap.

I lowered my head. Dad started with the opening lines of Rehraas Sahib. None of the words made any sense to me. I didn't see how this would help Mom. I kept my eyes fixated on the hospital floor until my mind began to see patterns in the grey and white speckles of the tiles.

***

My father's first instinct when anything happens, good or bad, is to pray. In instances when he is grateful and wants to celebrate, or when he faces situations that he feels he is helpless to change, he turns to prayer. In 1998, he prayed for Mom every day that she was in hospital. Back then, doctors were confused about what Mom's sickness was. Initially, they thought it might be pneumonia due to the blood that had collected and thickened in her lungs, but every medication they put her on failed to bring about the desired relief. The compounding effect of each new drug caused her weight and energy levels to fluctuate, and lowered the defenses of her immune system. Mom's condition worsened with each day. By the time doctors were able to correctly diagnose her as having a kidney disorder, her kidneys had lost ninety percent of their functionality. Mom was placed on dialysis and kept in hospital for weeks.

Dad didn't let me or Vijay know how dire Mom's prognosis was, or what stress he was going through. We didn't know if he was scared, hopeful, or if he felt anything. He wore the same expressionless face every time he took us to see Mom in the hospital. We knew Dad cared, otherwise he wouldn't have been at her side, but the lack of communication made him feel distant. Present, but distant. Dad tried to keep the household operating as smoothly as possible in Mom's absence and he asked me to keep up with my schoolwork. I stopped pretending that I was too sick to go to class. Mom's kidneys eventually improved, and she was allowed to continue her recovery at home. I learned years later that when Mom was still in hospital, Dad had been told by one of the doctors to look into making funeral arrangements. Dad believed it was the power of prayer that brought Mom back when we had almost lost her.

Despite recovering from her kidney failure, Mom still suffered from constant physical agony. Cracked bones, throbbing muscles, swollen feet, migraines with auras. Her bedside was a collection of Tylenol bottles, prescription meds, heating pads, and Dr. Ho's electrodes. The earliest instance I could recall something going wrong with her health was a few years before the kidney failure, back in the early nineties. I was too young to remember the specifics around it, but Mom had fainted in the living room while watching TV with the family. *Mahabharat* played on VHS in the background. Dad tried to pry her mouth open with a spoon so she wouldn't swallow her tongue. In my mind, I can still remember the sound of the metal spoon clinking against her teeth. That was just the beginning; after that, it seemed like there was a new pain Mom was coping with every few months. Often times, neither Mom nor her doctors could find a reason for the pain, and we would return home from hospital visits without any greater insight into how to soothe her discomfort. The pain became her default; it was the reason why, when people asked her how she was feeling, Mom didn't ever say she was doing well. Not wanting others to worry about her made her say that things weren't too bad.

When the recession hit in 2008, the window and door manufacturing company where Mom worked had shut down. She tried to lighten the financial burden from Dad's shoulders by working cash jobs with illegal employment agencies until she could find a permanent role, but there was too much instability. The location of the factory where she was assigned to work changed every week and sent her on bus routes that took her farther away from home. She didn't ever get paid on time either. Mom didn't have much work experience beyond the factories and meat packing plants she had occupied since she first arrived in Canada, and since the recession, steady labour jobs were becoming harder to find. Feeling defeated, Mom stopped working and decided to wait it out at home until the economy improved. That ended up being the last time she was ever employed.

Around 2010, Mom started to develop a painful growth in her mouth. The white splotches on her tongue initially made her sensitive to spicy foods. We stopped growing chili peppers in the backyard in the summers with our other vegetables, and she added less spice to her cooking. Over time though, her pain had progressed to a constant throbbing that no changes to her diet could salve. Her family doctor was unsure of what this was and didn't know how to treat it so he referred Mom to receive more specialized care at Sunnybrook Hospital. Upon examining her though, the staff at Sunnybrook were just as perplexed. The initial fear was cancer, but the tests done on the samples scraped from the inside of Mom's mouth came back negative. Her pain wouldn't stop though, and her condition worsened.

The first real diagnosis Mom received was that the growth in her mouth was just an ulcer, but the medications she was prescribed were ineffective. Doctors then said it was lupus, but changed their minds on that a few weeks after diagnosing her. Growing weary of Western medicine, my parents consulted with a few Indian homeopaths but none of their recommendations could remove the presence of the white sores which had expanded and coated the whole left side of Mom's tongue and the inside of her cheek.

At Sunnybrook, Mom was transferred from the department of dentistry, to dermatology, to otolaryngology, before landing in oncology. She didn't have cancer, but it was the closest category that her assortment of symptoms fit under. When Mom was finally diagnosed with cancer after several years of being treated by Dr. Higgins in the oncology ward, we felt a mix of relief and fear: relief that we finally had some clarity about what was going on with Mom's health and what the next steps in her treatment would be, and fear over not knowing how serious the cancer was and what recovery would look like.

In the few weeks that passed between Mom's cancer diagnosis and her scheduled surgery, the lump on the side of her neck had grown from the size of a marble to the size of a tennis ball. The night before the operation, Dad called Mom, Vijay, my nieces, my wife Nuvi, and me to sit together and pray as a family. I closed my eyes and tried to pay attention to the words as Dad led the prayer. I hoped that this—that we—would be able to help Mom.

***

Mom's operation began at 9:00 a.m. on a bright September morning and took ten hours to complete. Dad had taken the day off from work and spent the entirety of the procedure in the waiting room at Sunnybrook. I called him throughout the day to stay updated when I had breaks or slower moments during my shift with Unity Charity. When Dr. Higgins finally emerged from the operating room, he told Dad that things had changed.

Upon cutting Mom open, the team of doctors discovered that the stage two cancer that was present at the time of Mom's diagnosis just a few weeks ago had aggressively developed into stage four. It wasn't just localized in Mom's neck anymore either; the cancer had spread down her left shoulder and up her skull, stopping just short of her brain. Dr. Higgins said that he had to remove all nerves and blood vessels that emanated from around the tumour site.

At the conclusion of Mom's surgery, she was placed in a post-operation room until her condition stabilized. Visitation was restricted so I came straight home after work rather than joining Dad at the hospital. Even he only saw Mom for a few minutes after the operation before nurses told him to leave so that Mom could rest. Dad called me while he was on the way home from Sunnybrook and told me that when Mom had regained consciousness, she placed her palms together as an expression of gratitude that she had survived the procedure.

That night, a few hours after the completion of Mom's surgery, I sat on the couch in the basement and watched TV. It was a meaningless September baseball game between the Blue Jays and Orioles with neither team bound for the post-season. I had a hard time paying attention but I didn't want to go to sleep either. I kept thinking about Mom. The house felt empty again, like it did when she was taken to hospital back in 1998.

I kept the lights in the basement low and the volume of the TV down. Dad recited Kirtan Sohela upstairs, just as he did every night before he went to bed. When he finished, he joined me downstairs for the post-game show and sat on the other end of the couch. Neither of us spoke, our eyes fixated on the flat screen that hung above the fireplace. I wanted to ask him about Mom but he didn't know any more than I did at this point.

Dad didn't watch sports. Typically, if he made the effort to join me during something I enjoyed doing, it was because he wanted to talk to me about something he needed my help with, like a new project that he wanted to start up around the house or at his workplace. I had spent many weekends throughout my life at his furniture factory cleaning, painting, loading trucks, and building racking units.

"Was it a good game?" Dad asked.

I shrugged. "Toronto lost."

"Are you working tomorrow?"

I told him I would be. In addition to the job with Unity Charity, I had also started an internship at an agency that provided case management and counselling for people with mental health and substance use concerns. Dad always asked me a few perfunctory questions before he got to the heart of what he really wanted to talk about. I tried to focus on the post-game coverage and waited for Dad to get to the point. I noticed he held something in his hands but I couldn't make out what it was through the flickering of the television.

"Look," Dad said. He placed the objects on the couch in the space between us. I turned away from the TV to where he directed my attention.

"Are these...passports?" I asked. I picked up the navy blue booklets. The bindings were coming undone. The pages were frayed and turning brown. Inside were stamps that showed all of the places he had been and the lifetimes he had lived before he came to Canada, before he became my father. Sri Lanka, Sweden, Italy, Nigeria, Iran, Argentina, Japan, and many others. They were all there.

"You said you wanted to know," Dad said.

I looked up from the passports. My eyes met his. I noticed a hint of urgency behind Dad's gaze, like it wasn't just me who wanted to know about this part of his life, but that there was something within him that wanted to share these stories too.

I would soon learn that these passports were the keys to unlocking and understanding my father's life. These documents were the oldest records of our family's history, and the chronicle of how the waters from Dad's years at sea still overlapped with the shores of our present day lives.

I have only been to Punjab once in my life. I was in second grade in the winter of 1993. I remember being given a duo-tang full of homework sheets by my teachers Mrs. Guy and Ms. Lore in preparation for the trip to ensure that I stayed up to date with all the material the class would cover in the two months I would be away. All that I knew about Punjab before the trip was what I had learned from my parents: it was the language we spoke, the food we ate, the clothes we wore, the movies we watched, and the way we prayed. I remember being excited to go there and finally see where all of those things actually came from. I learned quickly that the place my parents recalled so fondly wasn't anything like our home in the Canadian suburb of Malton where we lived at the time. When a driver picked us up from the airport in Delhi to take us on the eight-hour drive to our village in Punjab, beggars surrounded our car in the night, banged on the windows, and asked for money. Some of them looked younger than I was. The driver inched the car forward through the crowd and refused to let the vehicle come to a complete stop.

During our trip, we stayed in Nawan Pind, a small farming village in the countryside of Punjab's Jalandhar district. The name Nawan Pind literally translates to 'new village,' but in the time I spent there, it felt old and untouched by time. It was the same village where Dad and his four siblings were born and raised. It was the same place where Dad's father—my Dhadha Ji, Dhanna Singh—was raised, as were his parents before him. Dad's younger brother Mohinder was the only sibling that still resided in the village. I spent most of my stay in Nawan Pind going back and forth along a dirt road that stretched from the family farm at one end to the village gurudwara at the other. Our home was situated in the centre between these two landmarks.

The verandah of Mohinder Chacha Ji's house in Nawan Pind was enclosed by grey stone walls and a white, sliding metal gate with blue diamond shapes painted across the top. Inside the verandah, flowers and vines snaked their way up from the ground to the tops of the stone walls. In one corner, to the left of the gate, was a rusty green pump used to bring groundwater up to the surface for drinking and washing. In the mornings, if it wasn't too cold, we would bathe next to the pump using a plastic cup to catch and throw water. Next to the pump was a shack with a corrugated metal roof and foot grooves positioned on either side of a hole in the ground. This was the home's only toilet.

Mohinder Chacha Ji parked his red tractor at the back end of the verandah by a wide hallway that led to the rest of the house. On the other side of the hallway was a clearing in the middle of the home that had no ceiling. After it rained, Sarabjit Chachi Ji would squat down and spread the accumulated rainwater with a straw broom to clean the tiled floor. She cooked in a corner on the other side of the clearing and tossed lentils and vegetables into a round metal pot to prepare dhaal or sabji.

Across from where Chachi Ji cooked was a cement staircase that led to the rooftop of the house. I would sometimes find Chacha Ji up there tinkering with the radios and motors he was hired to repair by other villagers, a side hustle he operated for some extra cash in addition to running the family farm. Most homes in the village were connected to each other which made it easy to hop from one rooftop to another and visit with neighbours. Some of them were farmers, others were tailors and seamstresses who sewed sweaters, women's clothing, and soccer balls. People were happy to see unexpected visitors and they greeted all who came to their door—or rooftop—with tea and snacks.

At the back of the family house was a living room that was painted teal. We would sit there on squeaky, brown leather sofas to watch Punjabi movies or the local news on a fourteen-inch colour television set with rabbit ears. We didn't always have power though; the lights went out every night, and we passed the time by huddling around a fire and roasting peanuts.

The back entrance of the house was covered by a tattered brown cloth that hung across the length of the doorway. Lifting the cloth took me out to the orange cobblestone alleyway behind our home. The alleys were like arteries that connected us to the other blocks in the village. Sometimes I explored on my own and ran my hand along the leaning brick walls of the houses that backed out onto the lanes. Open gutters flowed through the alleys and carried raw sewage. The smell and sound of a fresh fire crackling somewhere would permeate through the air.

My parents seemed more relaxed in Punjab. In Malton, they didn't want me and Vijay to ride our bikes too far from home. In Nawan Pind though, Mohinder Chacha Ji let us drive his mint green Bajaj Chetak scooter on our own, without supervision and without helmets. Vijay and I loved the freedom and adventure Punjab provided and we frequently took the scooter out for rides down the dirt road to the family farm. Vijay would sit in the driver's seat and steer, and I'd stand on the footrest in front of her. We dodged and maneuvered around cyclists, women walking with baskets balanced atop their heads, and men riding in wooden carts led by oxen. The other homes on our block on the way to the farm looked like they were built in patchwork; some houses had door and window frames that were reinforced with fresh cement, the dark and wet grey contrasting against the peeling and faded pink and yellow paint that some homes on the block were coated with.

Next to the houses was a sugarcane field. Vijay and I sometimes stopped the scooter, propped it on its kickstand, and ran inside the rows of green and yellow stalks that towered over us. We'd work together to pull a stalk out of the ground and used our teeth to tear strips of the sheath off. Sometimes we climbed the Chinese date trees next to the sugarcane. At the farm, male workers dressed in flip flops and button-up shirts with the collars flared out and the sleeves rolled up would scatter feed across the dark brown earth for chickens to peck at. Other farmhands milked cows that stood inside wooden pens. Mohinder Chacha Ji sometimes sat me on his lap and took me out on his tractor for a spin around the farmland. Fields of emerald green and golden amber crops were interspersed with patches of fresh soil lined with small tufts of newly-planted produce. In this part of the village, there weren't any homes or buildings to block our view; from the farm, the world seemed to stretch out endlessly in every direction.

The other end of this strip, away from the farm and the family home, was the village gurudwara. I remember it being very small. It was a one-level concrete building that was painted white and felt much different from the gurudwaras back home in Mississauga and Rexdale that were former schools or warehouses repurposed into places of worship. The gurudwara in Nawan Pind had no doors, only an entrance that led directly into the main hall where morning and evening prayers were held. My parents and I went there at least once a day. The gurudwara was where we mainly saw the other villagers. During the waking hours, people worked and were busy with their jobs and families, but they made it a point to come to the gurudwara to begin and end their days.

I enjoyed my time in Punjab. The people were open and welcoming. There were fewer rules and my parents seemed less guarded. I went hours without supervision and had the ability to come and go anywhere in the village as I pleased. The other villagers referred to me as 'Satnam's son.' Dad's name carried weight and commanded their respect. The days in the village moved slowly. People worked hard, but at their own pace. Even the breeze and the movement of the leaves on the trees felt unhurried. My ability to speak Punjabi improved much quicker than it did during the Saturday morning classes Vijay and I were enrolled in back in Malton. I didn't drink tea before coming to Punjab, but I grew an affinity for the way Chachi Ji made cha with cloves and cardamom. Vijay, and I drank Coke from glass bottles and spent hours playing a variation of hopscotch that involved kicking a wooden block between four squares drawn on the ground. I was sad to leave.

When we came back to Canada, I spoke exclusively in Punjabi with my uncles and aunties. I asked my parents to make long distance calls to Nawan Pind on a weekly basis so I could speak to Chacha Ji and Chachi Ji regularly. However, as I returned to school and my regular routine, over time, the excitement of the trip wore off. My Punjabi lost some of the precision of its pronunciation. I stopped wearing the home-made sweaters and jeans the other villagers had made for me. The simplicity of village life seemed farther away from my everyday reality in Canada. Some of my other classmates who went on vacation to Punjab with their families would return and joke about how behind the times their villages were. In Canada, we had reliable electricity, running water, toilets that we could flush, and video games. Canada was more advanced, we all agreed. What I didn't realize at the time though was that life in Nawan Pind as I had experienced it was a progression from the way my father grew up. It was a progress that he worked hard to achieve and it came at the cost of him being away from home for years at a time. The respect

Dad's name carried in the village was the result of him facing threats to his own freedom and mortality all for the sake of the betterment of his family.

***

I sat across the dinner table from my father. The black marble of the tabletop reflected the white light from the square fixture above us. Dad sat with his back to the sliding door. It was dark out and I couldn't see the trees in the ravine behind him. He was wearing an orange dastaar and an ivory white kurtha. His beard hung down to his chest; some slivers of grey and black hair still flowed among the whites.

"I guess we should start at the beginning," I said. Dad nodded. I set the passports down on the table in front of me.

As much as I wanted him to tell me the story of his life, we didn't really ever sit down with each other like this and just talk. For most of my life, Dad only spoke when he felt it was necessary, like when there was some job to be done. This type of communication didn't come naturally for us. It wasn't something we knew how to do. Dad was always involved in every birthday, family wedding, and summer barbeque, but like many elders in my family, he felt emotionally unreachable. His poise was like that of a stone statue: he was consistent in his presence and provided shade, but he didn't ever flinch.

"Dhadhi Ji always said you had two birthdays," I started. Dad's passport stated his date of birth was on October 10, 1953. My grandmother always said he was born closer to January though. "Which one is your actual birthday?"

"I don't know," Dad chuckled and waved a hand at me. He leaned back in his chair. "We didn't know that birthdays were supposed to be celebrated until we came to Canada."

"Why do you have two though?"

"Probably because we still used the Bikrami calendar back then."

Dad explained how documenting new births in Punjab in the fifties when he was born was the designated responsibility of government officials who would each travel between a dozen villages every few months. The lack of precision regarding exact birth dates came from the fact that Indian government employees and residents in urban areas used the standard Gregorian calendar introduced by the British, while most rural villagers still largely used the Bikrami calendar which had been in use long before that. Trying to approximate dates from one calendar system to another several weeks or months after a birth had actually taken place led to some information being lost in translation.

"How many brothers and sisters did Dhadha Ji and Dhadhi Ji have?" I asked. I felt embarrassed for asking such a simple question, one I felt I should have already known the answer to. I couldn't learn if I didn't ask, I assured myself. I was more familiar with my grandmother's side of the family. I had met most of her siblings. On my grandfather's side though, I didn't know anything about how he grew up.

"Your Dhadhi came from a family of four boys and four girls," Dad said. He explained that Dhadhi Ji and her siblings were all born in the village of Dhilwan in Punjab. Some of her siblings eventually left the village for other parts of the world. Her brothers Bachittar, Harbhajan, and Nirmolak all moved to Ontario in the seventies, first to Toronto and then into surrounding areas like Mississauga, Brampton, and Brantford. Her other brother Gurmukh[1] remained in Punjab until he passed away in the nineties. Her sisters Amarjit and Davinder lived with their children in California and Michigan, respectively.

"The eldest sibling was Jeeto," Dad said.

"Where does she live?" I asked. I hadn't heard of her before.

"She died in Punjab shortly after giving birth. I was very young then." Dad squinted his eyes as if he was searching for the scant memories of her that he still had. The only thing he could recall was a vague recollection of her washing clothes by a riverbed.

Dhadhi Ji was pulled out of school at a young age to work on her family's farm. Her parents taught her to greet every elder they saw in the village with respect regardless of what caste they belonged to. Any time a beggar visited the house, Dhadhi Ji washed the person's hands and feet with warm water, and provided them with either something to eat or clothes to wear. Dhadhi Ji's parents believed in hukam—divine will—and felt that if something was ever stolen from the house or from the farm, rather than getting upset, they trusted that they were chosen as vessels to provide for the less fortunate.

Dhadha Ji came from a family of five boys and two girls. His sisters Chanan and Resham moved to England and New Zealand with their husbands later in life. None of Dhadha Ji's brothers ever left Punjab.

---

1   Not to be confused with my father's cousin referenced in chapter one. Dad had both a cousin and an uncle named Gurmukh.

Dad couldn't remember much about Dhadha Ji's older brothers Darshan and Pritam. He told me Dhadha Ji's brother Amar had died when he was nine years old, burned to death as he played near an open flame on the farm. Dhadha Ji's younger brother Pyaara was also hurt on the farm, having been gored in the stomach by the horn of an ox. Trailing blood behind him as he walked back home to get help, Pyaara collapsed in the verandah and was taken to a hospital. He survived and lived to tell the story, the size of the ox and the amount of blood lost increasing with each retelling of the tale to draw the astonishment and wonder of the children in the village.

I thought of what to say next. I didn't know when Dad and I would have time to talk like this again with our attention soon turning to Mom's recovery. Dad didn't open up like this to me so I wanted to ask the right questions to learn as much about him as I could.

"How was Dhadha Ji as a father?" I asked.

Dad looked down. He kept his eyes on the white veins that flowed through the surface of the black marble table. "He was tough," Dad said. He shook his head. "He would disappear sometimes. He'd meet up with his friends and go somewhere. He didn't tell us where he was. He'd come back drunk. Sometimes he'd work with his brothers and they would make their own moonshine to sell to people in other villages."

"What was he like when he was drinking?"

"He would beat me. Not my sisters, but me and my brothers got it bad."

For what my father lacked in communication, he made up for in consistency. I didn't ever have to question where he was; I knew that if he wasn't at home, he was at work. I didn't grow up living under the threat of violence. The hollow clinking of empty alcohol bottles didn't soundtrack my upbringing the way it did for Dad. He chose to end that cycle for me.

"He used to hit your grandma too sometimes," Dad said. I noticed the muscles tightening in his face. He looked uncomfortable even saying the words. "There was one time that I can remember very clearly. I must have been five or six years old. He threw her to the ground. He had this wooden cane." I felt my lungs shrinking, like the breath was being forced out of my chest. "Every time she tried to get up, he hit her—in the legs, in the back," Dad described. "He knocked her around pretty bad. I don't remember what he was upset about."

Before both of Dad's parents passed away, for most of my lifetime, they were always bickering with each other about something. Dhadha Ji would tease Dhadhi Ji, get a rise out of her, and cackle to himself. Sometimes Dhadhi Ji would put her palms together and lower her head as a sign of defeat, pleading for mercy to get the torment to stop. When I was a kid, they just seemed like an old married couple that knew how to push each other's buttons and had grown cranky from spending too many decades together. I didn't know then that Dhadha Ji's behaviour was a mutation of the physical abuse he had put Dhadhi Ji through in their younger years that neither of their bodies could sustain in old age.

"She did a lot," Dad said of Dhadhi Ji. "My dad was on the farm all day, so it was mainly my mom that raised me. She did more than what society dictated women could do at that time, like managing the little bit of money the family got. She was busy doing some sort of task somewhere in the village at all times of the day."

When Dad was a child, Dhadhi Ji would visit the village gurudwara every morning before the rooster's caw signaled the arrival of the new day. She would then return and make roti for Dhadha Ji and the other farm workers. She made butter by hand and did a lot of the dirty work on the farm, milking cows and spreading their droppings on the crops as fertilizer. She flattened manure into discs and dried them out in the sun to make fuel sources to burn at home. She picked cotton from the fields and operated a hand-crank to separate seed from thread. She and the other women in the village would pool their thread together to make cotton fabric while reciting Gurbani or sharing stories of the daily gossip and happenings around the village.

Dad shared with me his most treasured memory of Dhadhi Ji from his childhood. They were walking home together from the family farm and the sun was just beginning its descent. Dad skipped along the dirt road and ran a few steps ahead of Dhadhi. When he looked back at her, she had the orange sun glowing behind her. Sunlight cascaded onto her shoulders. She held a baby in one arm, a bucket of milk in the other, and balanced a basket on her head full of clay dishes and dung fuel wrapped in cloth. Of all the things she carried, she didn't let any of them waver or fall to the ground.

"What was it like growing up on the farm?" I asked.

"I've been all over the world," Dad said. "I've seen a lot of different places and experienced the way people live." I felt like he was leaving more breadcrumbs again, dropping hints that exposed fragmented pieces of his past without sharing the larger picture. "Never in my life have I seen people live under stress the way they do here." The 'here' he referred to was Canada. "People will kill themselves by working long hours just to make a couple of dollars here."

I wasn't sure if Dad was criticizing the never-ending rat race that was the working world in the West, or if he was lamenting some of the decisions that he made in the past to survive within that system. Maybe he was talking about both. For as long as I could remember, he regularly worked six days a week—usually ten to twelve hours on weekdays, and eight hours on Saturdays. He didn't sleep for more than four or five hours a night. He was the first person who I saw work to exhaustion to make a few extra dollars even when his body and mind needed rest. Whenever I called in sick at school or work, Dad would poke fun at me and say young people weren't supposed to get tired or feel ill. He bragged about how he didn't miss a day of work regardless of how sick or hurt he was.

"How was Punjab any different?" I asked.

"Everything in Canada is about money. In the village, nobody really worked for money. Everything was based on trade. There wasn't much unemployment because you inherited your job from your family. Whether you were a carpenter, weaver, farmer, ironsmith, tailor, shoemaker, or water dispenser, each job had a purpose. Every person was dependent on everyone else in the village, so we worked for each other. If someone helped us out on the farm, we made sure we fed them for the day. When we harvested our crops, we shared with everyone else so they could eat too, or we gave them seeds to grow their own. People don't share or look out for each other like that in Canada."

I broke eye contact with Dad and looked at the clock on the microwave. The bright, green, digital numbers indicated that we had been talking for several hours. It was much later than when Dad usually went to bed on a weekday.

Dad looked at the clock as well. "We'll talk more soon," he said. He placed both palms against the dinner table and pushed himself up from his chair. "You should go to sleep too. You have work in the morning." He patted me on the shoulder and went off to bed.

I sat there alone for a moment and reflected on everything Dad had shared with me. I followed the grey and white lines of the dinner table and examined how they moved through the black marble. They looked like waves flowing around landmasses. I tried to imagine what it must have been like for Dad to grow up the way he did. I tried to picture what life was like, what the family was like, and what he was like, back then in a world before this world.

***

Satnam held his mother Sampuran's hand. He walked barefoot along the dirt road towards the gurudwara in Nawan Pind. He was seven years old.

"I really need to get you a new pair of shoes," Sampuran said. The footwear Satnam got from the village shoemaker didn't last more than a couple of months with all the running and tree-climbing he did. "It's going to be hot this afternoon. How will you walk home without shoes?"

"Don't worry about shoes," Satnam laughed. "There are these trees on the way to school. I rip off the biggest leaves I can find and tie them to my feet. I did that yesterday and the leaves protected me just as good as any shoes would."

Sampuran frowned. She moistened her thumb with saliva to wipe a spot of dirt from Satnam's red dastaar.

The painted white walls of the gurudwara's exterior came into view like a beacon through the grey morning fog. Satnam's classmates Jarnail, Dheba, and Boota stood outside the entrance of the gurudwara with their mothers. Satnam shook loose of Sampuran's hand and ran towards his friends. All four boys were identically clad in their school uniforms of khaki pants, white dress shirts, and red dastaars.

"Bye Ma," Satnam said. "We're going—"

"Aren't you forgetting something?" Sampuran interrupted. She adjusted the brown, cotton shawl draped around her shoulders. "Bow your heads inside before you go."

The boys stopped their banter and followed each other into the gurudwara. Sampuran waited outside and chatted with the other mothers. A few moments later, Satnam ran out of the gurudwara and hugged Sampuran, throwing his hands around her hips and burying his face in her abdomen.

"Okay, now we're going," he said.

"Be safe," Sampuran advised. She knelt down and cupped his cheek.

"Your dad needs your help on the farm after school today, okay?"

Satnam nodded and broke free of his mother's embrace. "I'll race you to school!" he called to his friends and ran off laughing. He turned back mid-stride and waved at Sampuran. The sight of his mother disappeared in the fog.

The four boys travelled shoulder to shoulder along this route to their elementary school in the neighbouring village of Nussi every day. The blush of the morning sky eventually caused the fog to fade. Along their journey, they passed by women walking with baskets balanced atop their heads, and men riding in wooden carts led by oxen. They passed by the sugarcane field where they sometimes ran inside the rows of green and yellow stalks that towered over them. They would work together to pull a stalk out of the ground and used their teeth to tear strips of the sheath off. Sometimes they climbed the Chinese date trees next to the sugarcane. They'd pass by Satnam's family farm where fields of emerald green and golden amber crops were interspersed with patches of fresh soil lined with small tufts of newly-planted produce. In this part of the village, there weren't any homes or buildings to block their view; from the farm, the world seemed to stretch out endlessly in every direction.

C.05
NO PRESSURE

My family arrived in Canada in waves. Dhadhi Ji's younger brother Bachittar Singh was the first to leave Punjab for Toronto in 1970. Their brothers Nirmolak and Harbhajan followed in '71 and '72 respectively. In 1973, Bachittar got married to Mom's sister, my Massi Ji Kulwinder Kaur. After becoming a Canadian citizen, Massi Ji sponsored Mom, Amarjit Mamma Ji, Nani Ji, and Nana Ji to join her in Canada, and they all arrived in March 1980. Mom and Dad got married in Punjab in December 1981, and Dad landed in Canada a few months later in February '82. Once Dad was settled, he sponsored his siblings and parents throughout the eighties and early nineties. Nobody was financially stable in Canada when they applied for sponsorship, but they still extended their hands back to Punjab to reunite the family one member at a time. In my mind, I likened them to trapeze artists who waited for their partners to leave their perch and surrender to the uncertainty of air alongside them.

My sister Vijay was born in June 1983, and my parents had me in December '86. As Vijay and I got older, our parents worried about how going to public school, entering the English-speaking world, and being socialized as Canadians would affect the way we connected with our Sikh and Punjabi roots. My parents didn't care much for participating in Western customs like Halloween and Christmas that they either didn't understand or didn't want to waste money on. To dissuade my excitement when I was young, my parents had told me that Christmas was only for Christians, and that Santa Claus didn't ever give us presents because we were Sikh. Cultural preservation was important to my family. They had left their physical homes behind—they didn't want to lose the pieces of home they brought to Canada with them.

Growing up, my parents made it a household rule that Vijay and I had to communicate in Punjabi with all elders in our family. They also limited what aspects of Western culture they allowed in the home. Part of that came from their upbringing in Punjab and the resistance of their parents' generation against British colonial influence. As a result, my parents referred to all styles of clothes, music, and movies that weren't traditionally Indian as being 'English.' Rap music, Hollywood movies, TV shows like *Married with Children* and *The Simpsons*—they each fell under the all-encompassing umbrella of English. However, there were moments when my parents needed me to use my English-speaking skills to manage situations that they didn't feel comfortable handling themselves. I remember being as young as ten years old and trying to muster as much bass in my voice as possible in hopes of convincing the cable company that it was really my father speaking to them on a service call.

To help Vijay and I sharpen our skills in our native tongue, our parents signed us up for Punjabi language classes on Saturday mornings. These classes were held in schools in our neighbourhood and took place from nine in the morning until noon. Other languages offered through the program included Urdu, Cantonese, Hindi, Italian, and many others from all around the globe.

Both inside and outside of the Saturday morning classes, growing up in an immigrant-heavy neighbourhood like Malton exposed me to other cultures and languages from an early age. Our neighbours were Italian on one side, Yugoslavian on the other, and we had two Jamaican families right across the street from us that I played baseball and basketball with. A Punjabi woman a few houses down gave me and Vijay rides to school sometimes when the winter mornings were too cold. Amarjit Mamma Ji's house was the next block over from us and his neighbours were a large Muslim family from India that had bought two houses on the same street. Other families on their block were Portuguese, Guyanese, Pakistani, and Costa Rican. In the summers, it was common to hear both Buju Banton and Jazzy B blaring from different car systems driving by.

Malton is located right next to Pearson International Airport. We saw planes flying overheard at all times of the day. Someone was always coming or going. Malton is a working class neighbourhood. Most of my friends and classmates in elementary school were from first-generation immigrant households who were still trying to establish themselves in Canada. Parents in Malton mostly did blue collar jobs as cabbies or truckers, or they worked in factories or at the airport. Workplaces looked just as mixed as the schoolyards did. It wasn't a racial utopia though. Most of the trepidation I experienced around living in a multicultural neighbourhood came from the older generations. I was warned multiple times by uncles and aunties in my family not to play with or visit the homes of other Black or Muslim kids in my class. I didn't pay their fears much mind though. At recess, we all joined in on soccer games together, traded pogs and hockey cards, and learned each other's slang and swear words. Among the kids I grew up with, we knew we were all culturally different from each other, but there was a unity in how we shared parts of our identities with one another.

Though the Saturday morning classes I was enrolled in were supposed to focus on reading, writing, and speaking Punjabi, the classes were poorly funded and organized if one wasn't old enough to be taking an international language class for a high school credit. All the kids from kindergarten to grade eight were shoved into the same classroom and the teachers had no way to cater to each student's existing literacy levels. To make the hours meaningful, some of my teachers often discussed the culture behind the language. We learned about Mata Khivi who helped to organize and spread the Sikh concept of langar—the community kitchen where volunteers prepared and served free food to everyone regardless of caste, socioeconomic status, gender, or race. We learned about Bhagat Puran Singh who established Pingalwara, a foundation that provided care to the sick, disabled, and dying who had nowhere else to go. We learned that so much of our history as Sikh and Punjabi people was rooted in giving to others.

Growing up, I sometimes overheard Dad and Gurmukh Thaya Ji engage in discourse about Gurbani over the phone. Dad once said that anyone who has a stomach to fill has worries, which makes us all beggars in life. We all ask the universe for more and more to the point that we lose sight of what we already have. The blessings we receive aren't just for ourselves, he explained; our gains are meaningless if we can't share in them.

Dad was the oldest of five siblings. His sister Jasvir Kaur was three or four years younger than him. He's not sure how much older he is than his brothers Mohinder and Sardara. The only age difference he can recall with any certainty is the seventeen-year age gap between himself and his youngest sister Kuldip. For their sake, Dad was forced to grow up quickly. As the eldest sibling, he played a parental role for them from an early age, acting as babysitter in between homework and helping his parents on the farm. In Punjab, as in Canada, Dad didn't consider the money he earned to be his own—it belonged to the family and it was meant to help everyone rise up. The influence from Sikh history that I learned in my Saturday morning classes, and the absorbed wisdom of my father's words helped guide the career path that I chose for myself. I wanted to do something that allowed me to give back and serve the community around me. Both jobs I was working in September 2017, with youth and in mental health, were a result of those influences.

The day after Mom's surgery, my supervisors at the mental health agency where I was doing my internship suggested I visit Grace United Church, which was one of our key community partners. Located in the heart of downtown Brampton, the staff there served free breakfast and lunch to whoever needed it. Just like Mata Khivi, I thought. I had driven by the church hundreds of times before and had seen groups of people hanging outside there in the mornings, but thought nothing of it. I assumed there was a bus stop by the church or that people were there to pray. What I learned that day though was that many of those people were homeless. When I entered the church and took the staircase down to the basement, I couldn't believe what I saw.

On the left side of the basement, behind a table where volunteers took names on a sign-up sheet of everyone who came to eat, were people sleeping on beds. Some of them used their backpacks as makeshift pillows and their jackets as improvised blankets. To the right were rows of plastic tables that stretched from one end of the room to the other. Each table was draped in a red and white checkerboard tablecloth. People of all ages and ethnicities sat at the tables with their plates filled with chicken breast, greens, and pasta. There must have been over a hundred people there. Forks and spoons clattered against dishes. People talked and laughed between bites of food. Young girls adorned in black hijabs who were volunteers from a local Islamic school wheeled carts down each row and served juice and cake for all those who attended.

I stood at the back of the room by the stacks of extra tables and folding chairs and watched everything. I didn't want to get in the way.

I felt that this job was going to be hard. I didn't know what it was like to be unsure of where my next meal was coming from. I didn't see what I could say or do or offer that would help. Whenever I visited downtown Toronto, homelessness was more apparent. It was hard to ignore the people who slept on sewer grates to absorb the heat that rose upward from underground, or the people who sat cross-legged outside of restaurants and subway stations and asked for spare change. I didn't see homelessness like that in Brampton, or in any suburb for that matter, but here it was in my own backyard, and in numbers that were far greater than I could have imagined.

When I left the church and returned to the office, my first thought was to feel sorry for the people I saw in there. They needed support though, not pity. They weren't sad or quietly eating their meals—there was laughter and community. They shared with each other and talked about where they wanted to go in life. They were fighters, resilient in the face of a society that made assumptions about who they were. I thought about how when it appeared that all had been lost, a house of God was always open.

***

In the days after Mom's surgery, visitation to see her in the recovery room at Sunnybrook was heavily restricted. Even Dad was only allowed to see her for a few minutes a day before nurses sent him home. Mom's immune system was weakened, so having too many people around put her at risk for further illness and caused her blood pressure to spike. Dad kept me up to date though and told me that Mom was doing well. A few days after the operation, Mom's condition had stabilized to the point that doctors moved her from the recovery room to a bed in the cancer ward. She was allowed to have more visitors now.

One evening after work, my wife Nuvi and I travelled with Dad to see Mom at Sunnybrook. Dad drove and I sat behind the passenger seat where Nuvi was. A light rain drizzled against the windshield and made the lights from the cars around us appear as blurs of yellow and red in the night. I wanted to continue the conversation that I had started with Dad a few days ago but I wasn't sure how to bring it up. As our car climbed the ramp to transition from highway 410 to the 401, Dad was the one that chose to share more of his past.

"Did I ever tell you about the floods when I was a kid?" Dad asked over his right shoulder. His face was covered in shadows as he drove, and he only became illuminated by a brief flash of orange light when we passed under one of the towering lampposts that lined the side of the highway.

"No, I don't think you did," I said. There was a lot about his life that I hadn't heard about.

"I was about eight years old. One year, we had a really bad monsoon season. Rain for days and days like you couldn't imagine—not like the rain we get here. Some of the villages that were on lower land got flooded out. They looked like they had totally disappeared from the map. People who lived in those areas had to swim or use planks of wood like rafts to get to safety."

"How close were the floods to Nawan Pind?" I asked.

"The floods were *in* Nawan Pind," Dad chuckled.

"Our village got flooded?" I leaned forward so I could hear him better, poking my head into the space between the two front seats. "What did you do?"

"It was hard," he said. "Very hard."

During Dad's childhood, his family home, and most of the other houses in Nawan Pind, were built with bricks made out of mud. The walls were a few feet thick to keep the elements out, which created a cool haven inside away from the burning gaze of the sun. Dad spent the early part of his life in a home that was about twenty feet wide and forty feet long. The roof of the home was constructed with severed tree trunks that were laid horizontally across the tops of the walls. The gaps between the trunks were bridged with branches, leaves, and long blades of grass to provide shade. Soil and rocks were placed on top of the branches to anchor them in place.

When the monsoon hit in the early sixties, Dad's home was destroyed. Gusting winds ripped the grass and branches off the top of the house. The walls of the home were knocked over and the rain caused the mud bricks to liquefy. The rain had accumulated so much that the wells that plunged deep into the earth to retrieve groundwater were now filled to the brim and overflowing. Dad was homeless in the only place his family had called home for centuries.

"It wasn't just us," Dad continued. "There were five or six other families from our village that had their homes torn down as well."

"Where did you go from there? Did you stay with relatives?" Nuvi asked.

"The gurudwara was the only building in the village that was made out of concrete," Dad said. "It was on higher ground than the rest of the houses too, so we joined the other families there."

The gurudwara sat next to the house of the sarpanch, the elected community leader of the village. The sarpanch had a battery-powered radio and loudspeaker that broadcasted the news from Delhi for an hour every evening. The radio was the only contact that Nawan Pind had with the rest of India, and all the villagers would huddle around the speaker to listen to the daily news. In the flooding though, the loudspeaker had fallen silent. The pattering of rain against the roof of the gurudwara was the only sound to be heard.

"It rained so much that we couldn't farm," Dad said. "The soil was completely waterlogged."

"What did you do for food?" I asked. After what Dad had told me about how integral the farm was to the village, being unable to grow crops would have impacted more families than just those who had lost their homes in the flooding.

"Wheat took a longer time to go bad than other crops, so we could still make roti," Dad explained. "We took all of our wheat to the gurudwara with us. We had to ration it so we wouldn't finish it too quickly. To help us create a more stable food supply, your grandfather and some of the other men went to villages that weren't as badly hurt by the floods and asked for food."

Dhadha Ji was proud, brash, and loud. I couldn't picture him begging anyone for anything. In his last few years before he died, he couldn't walk on his own anymore, but he didn't want anyone to help him get around. He would try to walk by supporting himself against walls or the headboard of his bed, but his legs weren't as strong as they used to be and he fell over frequently. If a few days had passed between my visits with Dhadha Ji, it was common for me to find him with new purple bruises and carpet burns on his hands, knees, and face. He wanted to feel like he was still living on his own terms, that he was still in control. In the defiance I had witnessed Dhadha Ji carry until his death, I couldn't imagine him asking anyone for help—but then again, I didn't know how the prospect of starvation could make one react.

"They asked other villagers if they could donate blankets or make food for us," Dad added. He smoothed his beard against the front of his navy blue coat. "They asked people if there were any jobs that needed to be done at their homes or on their farms. They traded labour for food. They did what they had to do. For survival."

I nodded to myself and tried to envision what it would have been like to lose the security and safety of the home we had. With Mom in the hospital, it didn't feel much like home anymore. In the uncertainty around her future though, at least the house was still physically standing; the roof wasn't collapsing, the walls weren't caving in, the floor wasn't crumbling beneath our feet.

Dad exited the highway and turned right onto Bayview Avenue. We were almost at the hospital, but I didn't want him to stop talking yet. There was still more I wanted to know.

"How long did you live in the gurudwara?" I asked.

"We were there for about two months."

Dad was only a child then. His younger sister Jasvir would have been about four years old at the time. They had other people who lived in the family home with them who also had to seek refuge in the gurudwara. In addition to Dhadha Ji and Dhadhi Ji were also Dhadha Ji's parents and Chacha, and his brothers Darshan, Pritam, and Pyaara. There were many mouths to feed and not enough food to sustain them all.

Dad explained that once the rain stopped, rebuilding the homes in Nawan Pind took another two months to complete. Villagers used metal, rectangular molds in which they placed slabs of mud to forge new bricks. They had to wait for every brick to dry out in the sun before they could stack them up.

"Nothing was ever the same after that," Dad said.

"What do you mean?" I asked.

"The floods came back every monsoon season for six years in a row. Our home was torn down each year. We had to go back to live in the gurudwara every time."

When it appeared that all had been lost, a house of God was always open.

"We had nothing," Dad noted. He parked the car on Sunnybrook property. "But when the rain stopped, we rebuilt again."

Dad, Nuvi, and I entered the main building of the hospital. I hadn't seen it so empty and dark before. Nobody was waiting in line for the elevators. Trace smells of pizza and coffee from the closed cafeteria hung faintly in the air. We didn't even come across any nurses in our walk to the cancer ward. It felt like everyone had gone home.

We paused in the doorway of Mom's room before entering. I looked inside and could barely see her. Her face was cloaked by the night and only partially lit up by the moonlight that came in from her room's window. Dad stepped aside and motioned with his hand for me to go in first.

"Sat sri akal, Mom," I said. I put my hands on her feet.

I looked over at the extensive system of tubes attached to her that were now responsible for all of her major biological functions. Fearful of inadvertently stepping on a tube or unplugging a machine tasked with keeping her alive, I didn't want to get too close. Long rows of stitches lined Mom's left shoulder. Staples ran across her neck from ear to ear and marked where the surgeons carved into her. Her hair was dry and disheveled. A thick tracheal tube was placed over the surgically-inflicted hole in her throat and carried a continuous flow of oxygen to her lungs. Mom had a strip of masking tape placed under her left collar bone with the words 'No Pressure' scrawled on it in black marker; it was a message left by nurses to notify the rotating hospital staff not to put any weight on Mom's chest. Mom tried to speak to greet us but the breath in her lungs escaped through the hole in her windpipe before she could form any words.

We only stayed with Mom for about fifteen minutes before Dad decided we should leave to let her rest. I don't remember if anyone spoke during the car ride home. I was too wrapped up in my own thoughts. Dad had been telling me that Mom was recovering well, but nothing I saw that night looked like recovery. This was just the first battle in the long war against cancer. We didn't know how dark and cold of a winter we were in for.

LIVE OFF THE LAND

CHAPTER ———— SIX

For centuries, farming in Nawan Pind and many parts of rural Punjab was primarily a way to keep the bellies of everyone in the village full, or to use as currency in trade with other professionals. During Dad's childhood though, India's position in a post-partition world led to a shift in the economics of farming. Agriculture was no longer just an ancestral trade that was passed down from generation to generation; farming had become more industrialized. Dad's world went from one that had very little use for money, to one where everything was dependent upon money. He told me that in the sixties, around the time the floods hit Nawan Pind, the Indian government introduced a middleman system that prohibited consumers from purchasing crops directly from farmers' fields; instead, farmers could only sell their produce to government-approved agents who would in turn sell the items through government-organized markets.

The intention behind the middleman system was to benefit farmers by setting fair and stable prices for their goods in the marketplace. This would allow them to earn enough money to purchase farming equipment and seeds to help prepare for the upcoming season. However, Dhadha Ji rarely used the money he received from his crop sales in ways that suited the needs of the entire family. Dad shared a story with me about how Dhadha Ji had at one point earned close to a hundred rupees through the sale of his crops to agents, but decided to spend nearly half of the profits on alcohol.

Despite Dhadha Ji's financial mismanagement though, the agents were not without fault either. Dad explained that it was common for agents to purchase crops from farmers at low prices, sell the produce at inflated rates, and pocket most of the profits for themselves. The system lacked transparency as it wasn't publicly known how prices were set. For poor and small-time farmers like my grandfather who had no awareness of what fair market prices were and felt powerless going against the government to ask for a bigger cut, they were kept blind to the fact that they were being paid a small fraction of what they actually should have been earning.

To help pay for the seeds and machinery that he initially failed to purchase with the money from his crop sales, Dhadha Ji procured finances from private lenders. Dad explained to me that it was easier to get money from a private lender than a bank back then. The danger though was that the interest rate on a loan shark's money could range anywhere from thirty to sixty percent. With each successive season, the money that Dhadha Ji earned from the sale of his crops was mostly put towards paying back the interest he owed on his loans rather than purchasing the resources he needed to continue farming. This trapped the family in a cycle of debt. Within India, other large-scale changes were also occurring in parallel to the introduction of the middleman system. These changes were known as The Green Revolution, and its impacts would be felt in Punjab and the world over.

***

The more Dad shared his story with me, the more past instances in my life began to crystallize and make sense within the larger picture of our family's migration. These were moments that showed me that despite being in Canada for decades, we were still very much tied to the people and the land of Punjab, and we were still figuring out how to make life work in both of the places we called home. Even the typical hallmarks of coming of age in North America, like getting my first car, were linked to my family's migration.

The first car I ever called my own was an olive-green 2002 Lincoln LS. It was the winter of 2006 and I was in my third year at McMaster University. Mom didn't ever get her driver's license, and Vijay was married and had moved out of the family home at the point, so we only had one car in the household which belonged to Dad. Up until then, I took the bus to get to and from university. Door to door, the commute took me three buses and two hours each way to travel between our house in Brampton to the school's campus in Hamilton. If I had class early enough in the morning, Dad would drop me off at the bus station after he dropped Mom off at work, which helped shave an hour off my trip.

The LS used to be Dad's car, but I ended up inheriting it from him that December due to circumstances we hadn't accounted for. One morning, when we made a left turn onto Stafford Drive in Brampton where Mom's factory was, the front wheel on the passenger side of the LS came completely off. The car collapsed with a thud into the pavement, spitting orange sparks in the face of the dark winter morning. Dad wound up buying himself a used car that was a few years old, and I got the LS when it was repaired and came out of the shop.

Shortly after Dad got his car, he asked me to help make the payments on it for a few months. Dad had asked me to help out with bills before, but he mostly told me to save my money for university. When I asked him if the family was doing okay financially, he explained that he had taken out a loan to send money back to Punjab. Dad said that he and Dhadhi Ji had been sending money to support Mohinder Chacha Ji in Nawan Pind since the nineties. Mohinder Chacha was the only one of Dad's four siblings who still lived back in the village and still farmed on the same plot of land that Dad helped tend to when he was a kid. Mohinder Chacha was struggling to make enough money to keep the farm running while also paying back the cash he owed to private lenders. The money Dad and Dhadhi Ji had been sending back to the village for years helped to keep Mohinder Chacha afloat.

A few days after Dad and I had the talk about finances, my parents and I visited Amarjit Mamma Ji's house in Brampton for my cousin Savraj's birthday just before Christmas 2006. Social events like birthdays and weddings in my family were usually separated along gender lines. Aunties and uncles all greeted each other warmly and caught up on the latest in health, work, and spirituality, but after that, it was typical for the men to sit with the men, and the women to sit with the women. Conversations among the men tended to focus on politics, both in North America and in India. Immigration, education, language rights, religious freedoms; these topics weren't just points of debate for them, but rather the foundational bricks that made up their identities and values. For my family, the personal was political, so we always had to be informed.

The older I got, the more my uncles considered it a rite of passage to allow me and my other male cousins to sit with them. I didn't always understand the topics of discussion as deeply as my uncles did, but the passion and animation in their responses as the conversations played out at least made it an entertaining environment to be in.

At Savraj's birthday, the men sat in the living room at Mamma Ji's house. Some of them drank alcohol, some of them didn't. Some of them leaned back in the white leather sofas, and others sat in chairs that had been dragged over from the dining table to accommodate everyone and form a circle. A rectangular wooden table covered with unfolded Punjabi newspapers and small white bowls filled with an assortment of nuts sat in the centre of the room.

"The Green Revolution took Punjab away from healthy living," Harbhajan—my Dhadhi's youngest brother—said as I walked into the living room. I had spent most of the evening with my cousins playing video games in the basement but decided to get a snack and join the uncles upstairs. The competing aromas of warm roti, rice, saag, and butter chicken floated into the room from the kitchen. All the other uncles nodded in agreement with Harbhajan. I sat in an empty chair next to Dad and tried to catch up on where they were in the discussion.

The Green Revolution marked a change in farming practices in the mid-sixties in many of parts of the world including India, Mexico, and several countries in South America, Africa, and Asia. All of the households in my family were farmers. For those that were alive in the sixties, they knew what farming was like before and after The Green Revolution.

There were several factors behind the introduction of The Green Revolution in India. Though Nawan Pind had experienced flooding throughout the sixties, India as a whole experienced a drop in national grain production in the middle of the decade due to drought. The state of Bihar—another region in India that, much like Punjab, was driven by agriculture—saw over a thousand deaths in the mid-sixties resulting from drought and starvation. To combat food deficits, the Indian government increased their food imports from other parts of the world, though over time, it became more expensive to continue importing. Mainly pushed by multinational corporations as a strategy to help ward off famine, The Green Revolution was the marriage of nature and technology where sweeping changes were made to how farming had traditionally been done. Genetically modified and disease-resistant high-yielding varieties (HYV) of wheat and rice seeds were introduced to increase agricultural productivity and reduce India's reliance on foreign food imports. Irrigation systems were developed on farms to allow farmers to grow more water-intensive crops outside of monsoon season. Farmers also applied more synthetic fertilizers and pesticides to help manage their crops.

"People didn't know how to use the chemicals they were buying," Bachittar Massar Ji added. Amarjit Mamma Ji sat next to him and set his whiskey glass down on the table, the ice cubes rattling against each other. He scooped a handful of cashews from one of the bowls.

"How could we? We weren't told by anyone what a safe amount of fertilizer or pesticide was," Dad said. "They made us use chemicals for everything. To fight off mosquitoes, we were told to use DDT. We didn't know how bad that was until years later. It hurt the poor farmers the most." Dad crossed his arms over his chest. "For hundreds of years, we didn't ever need chemicals to farm. To buy the new seeds and chemicals though, people had to take out loans. If you didn't have money to begin with, you just got stuck with debt."

"And look at what's going on now," Harbhajan replied. "There are water shortages—"

"What kind of future is there for farmers?" Massar Ji interjected. The room went quiet. Dad looked at the floor and shook his head.

It took me a few years to contextualize all the information I heard that night, but the conclusion I came to was that Dhadha Ji—and in turn Mohinder Chacha Ji—were casualties of The Green Revolution. Whatever successes these new changes in agriculture had in increasing grain supplies in the sixties, decades of using chemicals, buying HYV seeds, and tapping into groundwater supplies faster than could be replenished by rain was unsustainable. Over time, the harvests in Nawan Pind got smaller. The soil had become less fertile and couldn't return the sweat that was sowed. Mohinder Chacha took out loans to try to keep the farm operating. The money Dad and Dhadhi Ji sent back to Nawan Pind was the only way the debts stayed paid.

"Shall we go eat?" one of the uncles said, breaking the silence.

"Everything smells great," another uncle replied.

Dad poured his food and returned to his seat. He balanced his plate on his lap, closed his eyes, lowered his head, and said a quick prayer to give thanks, just as he did before every meal he ate.

Listening to Dad and my uncles talk that day, I learned about the hidden human cost of food, and how even the things we eat are political. Gaining that insight helped me understand why Dad was grateful for every morsel of food that crossed his plate.

***

The fallout of The Green Revolution is still being felt today. There is currently a suicide epidemic going on in Punjab. Data from Punjab Agricultural University shows that at least seven thousand Punjabi farmers committed suicide between 2003 and 2018. Among Indian farmers, the suicide rate is fifty percent higher than the national average. Many of the farmers who took their own lives shared several characteristics with my family: they were subsistance farmers with less than ten acres of land, and they could not earn enough money through farming to pay back the loans they had borrowed from private lenders and banks. As their debts grew, they saw death as being their only escape from this cycle.

When my uncles said that The Green Revolution took Punjab away from healthy living, they were right. Critics of The Green Revolution have stated that in the desperation to counter drought and famine in the sixties, the Indian government did not educate farmers on the health risks associated with using the agrochemicals required to grow HYV seeds. Studies from Punjab show that higher cancer rates are found in farming villages that use large amounts of pesticides. History does not exist in the past, but in the present.

***

Satnam stood next to his father Dhanna at the train station in Kartarpur. He was twelve years old. They were joined on the platform by Dhanna's sister Chanan, her husband Nazar, and their sons Gurmukh, Makhan, and Charanjit.

A crowd of travellers stood on the platform with them. Some craned their necks above the crowd to see when the next train would pull in. Mothers held babies on their hips. Friends hugged each other goodbye.

Chanan adjusted the white chunni on her head and used her elbows to push back against the crowd that was bumping into her and the family's brown leather suitcases. Their luggage was tied tight with yellow nylon rope, and a knot of colourful fabric was attached to the suitcase handles to help them differentiate their belongings from the others. The sun hung low and blazed the sky with a melting shade of orange. A hot breeze blew through the air.

Boxed in by the bodies around him, Satnam couldn't feel the wind from where he stood in the centre of the crowd. Each inhale of the humid air felt thick and heavy, carrying with it the smell of smoke emitted from the trains, and sweat from the densely-packed crowd. Satnam tugged on the sleeve of Dhanna's kurtha and asked when the next train was coming: ten minutes remained. Ten minutes until Gurmukh would leave with his family on a train bound for the airport. Satnam knew the day was coming when Gurmukh would have to join his father in Derby, but he didn't think it would come so soon.

"You should come with us, boy" Nazar said through bared teeth. Satnam smiled back and hoped it would hide the sadness he felt behind his eyes.

Nazar patted Satnam on the shoulder and turned to Dhanna. "I'm serious," Nazar began. "Come join us. What's left for you here? I hear the government's making a mess of things these days."

"They say the new seeds will help," Dhanna replied. He scratched his cheek through his thick black beard. The sweat glistening on his forehead soaked through the front of his blue parnaa. "We'll just have to give it time. We could really use the money."

Satnam looked up at both men and listened.

"Figure out your paperwork and come to England," Nazar said to Dhanna. "I can try to get you a job at the foundry." He raised a hand to his eyebrows as a visor to shield against the sun. Beads of sweat descended down his temples.

"I don't even have a passport," Dhanna retorted. "And what do I know about a foundry? I'm a farmer."

"I hear you're doing a lot less farming now."

Shortly after Nazar had first left Punjab for the UK in 1963, Dhanna began working at the airport for the Indian Air Force (IAF) in Adampur doing security and general building maintenance. In the aftermath of the first few floods in Nawan Pind, he needed money; relying on farming alone was only driving the family deeper into debt. Dhanna didn't have much experience in repairing fences, sewage lines, septic tanks, and drainage systems, and he knew even less about the military or aviation, but outside of farming, a military base was one of the few places where a young, able-bodied man with limited education could get steady work in Punjab.

Every morning, Dhanna rode his bicycle twenty kilometres from Nawan Pind to be among the roaring jet engines and bustling environment of IAF servicemen and pilots-in-training in Adampur. Military tensions between India and Pakistan had ramped up throughout Dhanna's tenure at the airport and culminated in the Indo-Pakistani War of 1965. In addition to being the largest tank battle seen since World War II, the war marked the first time the Indian and Pakistani air forces engaged in combat with each other since partition. People who lived close to the border between the two nations were told not to light any fires or turn on any lights after dark; doing so would make them targets for opposing planes to drop bombs on. One night during the war, when Satnam had stayed over at Gurmukh's house in Sangal Sohal, a Pakistani jet flew so close overhead that Satnam was certain the bombs would soon rain down. The plane was looking to shell an underground bunker just a few kilometres away from Nawan Pind where the Indian military was storing munitions but missed the target.

"My work with the air force isn't long-term," Dhanna said. "It's just for now until I can pay a few people back." He earned eighty rupees a month while working with the IAF. It wasn't much, but he needed whatever he could get his hands on to help pay down his debts and purchase new farming supplies.

Dhanna looked away from Nazar towards the direction of the bells clanging in the distance. The chk-chk-chk of the steamer's travel along the tracks grew louder as the train approached.

"Well, if you ever change your mind, give me a call," said Nazar. He and Dhanna shook hands.

Satnam turned away from his father and uncle and faced Gurmukh. "Promise you'll write me letters when you get to England?" Satnam asked. He barely got the words out past the knot that grew in his throat. He saw Gurmukh's mouth move in response but he couldn't hear what was said, his voice buried under the train's whistle that pierced the air.

Only a year apart in age, Satnam and Gurmukh were cousins but considered each other to be brothers. On holidays and breaks from school, Gurmukh would travel the fifteen kilometres either by foot or by bicycle to Nawan Pind to spend several nights at a time at Satnam's house, or vice versa with Satnam visiting Gurmukh in Sangal Sohal. Exploring neighbouring villages, and playing cricket, soccer, and gulli danda with the other village kids, Satnam and Gurmukh were best friends. Satnam appreciated having a relative close in age that he didn't have to babysit or keep watch over. Their parents trusted them both enough to allow them to roam about unsupervised as long as they were together. That was all changing now though. Satnam didn't want Gurmukh to leave.

The chatter among the crowd grew louder. People jostled for position on the platform to be among the first to board the train. Chanan pushed harder with her elbows to give herself more room against the restless crowd that encroached on her space.

"Boys!" Nazar called out. "Our train is here."

Dhanna held Satnam's hand and walked him across the width of the platform away from the tracks. Satnam turned his head and tried to locate Gurmukh amid the hundreds of people who funnelled onto the train but couldn't find him. Tears welled in Satnam's eyes; he wiped them away before Dhanna could see. The train let off a last whistle before pulling away from the station.

Gurmukh was gone. Europe seemed so far to Satnam that it may as well not have existed. Little did he know though that the repercussions of The Green Revolution would soon become a deciding factor in forcing him to seek out a life in Europe as well.

CH.07 CADILLACS & ALASKA

Looking after Mom in the days following her surgery required the efforts of the whole family. She was only allowed two visitors at a time in her room in the cancer ward, but we frequently had five or six of us in there with her. The aunties and uncles in my family didn't care much for Western rules that limited where, when, and how many of us could spend time together. We all wanted to be there for Mom as a show of support. Mom still couldn't speak but we learned how to make language out of her hand signals and facial expressions. We made sure to have at least one family member on site with her at all times to help her communicate with hospital staff.

My sister Vijay and I divided day duty at the hospital with Kulwinder Massi Ji and Bachittar Massar Ji. Sometimes Sardara Chacha Ji or Amarjit Mamma Ji or Kuldip Bhua Ji would stop by after work to see how Mom was doing. Mom never had a shortage of caregivers during the daytime. Dad volunteered to do the night shifts at the hospital alone, taking on the most difficult hours of the day so no one else had to. He took a few weeks off work so he could be there for Mom full-time after the surgery. Dad would usually get to the hospital for 5:00 p.m. and wouldn't return home until 9:00 a.m. the next morning. Vijay and I told him that we could alternate nights with him, and that he couldn't be much of a caregiver if he didn't also prioritize his own rest. Dad chose to be by Mom's side and saw it all as seva—the Sikh principle of selfless service to benefit others.

On the first Saturday after Mom's surgery, Vijay pulled her car into the parking lot at Sunnybrook and parked next to Dad. He stood outside his car and leaned against the hood. He had his face up and his eyes closed to absorb the sunshine. The mid-September morning teetered between late summer and early autumn—still bright and warm, but the wind carried with it the chill of a looming winter. Green and yellow leaves from the trees that dotted the hospital grounds swayed and rustled in harmony with the wind. I got out of Vijay's passenger seat to greet Dad.

"How's Mom doing?" I asked. Dad lifted himself up from the hood of the car.

"Better than before," he nodded. His response sounded cautious but optimistic.

Dad looked well put together, wearing an orange dastaar, and brown pants with a matching blazer over a white button-up shirt. His eyes looked tired though, like his wrinkles had sunken deeper.

"Did you get any sleep?" Vijay asked.

"A little bit." Dad pressed both of his hands into the small of his back and tilted his hips forward. "Hard to sleep in those hospital chairs."

"Go home and try to get some rest," I said. "We've got it from here."

Dad nodded. Vijay and I watched him get in his car and leave the parking lot.

"I'm worried about him," I said. I tracked his car as it waited at the traffic lights to exit hospital property. "He looks exhausted."

"I know," Vijay responded. "He won't ever admit it though."

Dad's car turned onto the road and sped out of sight.

Our day with Mom started off peacefully. She looked more alert and could walk the handful of steps from her bed to the toilet in her room. Vijay helped her clean and wash up. Nurses came by and made friendly banter with us, telling us how well Mom was recovering and what a pleasure she was to work with. Mom slept for most of the day as I read a book to myself by her bedside.

Suddenly, Mom's chest rattled. She let out a series of deep, heaving coughs. She couldn't breathe. Her face was turning red. I ran into the hall and called out to the nurses. Two of them rushed in. One of them said something about an obstruction in the tracheal tube. Mom's face looked swollen and turned a bruised shade of purple. The oxygen eluded her. Her torso arched up and flattened back down. Her legs kicked out from underneath her blanket. Her arms flailed, reaching out for anything that could save her. One of the nurses held Mom's shoulders down to restrain her. The other one shined a flashlight into the hole in Mom's throat and pulled out an assortment of bloody tubes. Seconds stretched into eternity. Vijay watched on in tears. I tried my best to swallow the lump in my throat all the way down to my stomach. I wanted to be the same rock in the storm for Mom that Dad was. The nurses steadied Mom's breathing. The blood drained from her face; she looked like herself again. Mom soon fell asleep as if the entire ordeal had never happened.

As much as Vijay and I were told that Mom was recovering well, it was a shaky peace. Any moment of calm couldn't be enjoyed because we were too worried that it would be snatched away from us.

***

Bachittar Massar Ji was the first one from my family to make the move from Punjab to Canada, but I didn't know why. When he came to visit Mom at the hospital that weekend, Massar Ji and I scheduled time where I could come over to his and Kulwinder Massi Ji's home in Mississauga to learn more. Dad's journey out of Punjab was incomplete without also learning how it connected to Massar Ji's story.

Growing up, my parents and I visited with Massar Ji and Massi Ji regularly. In the summers, we played basketball and barbequed in their backyard. We watched professional wrestling at their house and cheered on the likes of Randy Savage and Bret Hart over villains like Yokozuna and Papa Shango. Massar Ji would wrestle with me when I was a child, twisting my legs like pretzels into complicated submission holds. Behind a smile that lifted his rosy cheeks and narrowed his eyes, he encouraged me to escape. Other times, he would position himself on all fours and I crawled on his back. With my arms wrapped around his shoulders, I would try to tackle him to the floor but he wouldn't budge.

Massar Ji had a serious side too. Dad deeply respected and admired him, and they spoke at length about Gurbani. Much like Dad, Massar Ji was involved in every family occasion, but he too felt emotionally unreachable. They both felt guarded, like they couldn't ever reveal too much of what they were thinking or feeling. Why Massar Ji came to Canada and what his early years here were like weren't parts of himself that he spoke about openly, so I was surprised when he agreed to meet with me to talk about it.

I rang the doorbell of Massar Ji and Massi Ji's two-storey Mississauga home and stood on the concrete step that led up to the front door. Grey stones on the lawn outlined flowerbeds where withering purple, yellow, and red flowers surrendered to autumn. Massi Ji's toothy smile beamed through the screen door as she answered the bell. She radiated a welcoming and positive energy.

"Welcome, Amrit!" She swung the door open and reached an arm out towards me.

"Sat sri akal, Massi Ji," I smiled back and hugged her.

"Come. Your Massar Ji is waiting for you."

She led me into the living room where Massar Ji sat on a tan loveseat that was framed by dark, brown wood on the armrests and atop the backrest. Wearing navy blue slacks, a white dress shirt, and a dastaar that matched his pants, he raised a hand to shake mine. His long silver beard was neatly tied in a small knot at the bottom of his chin. Massi Ji sat across from him on a round, grey ottoman with her legs crossed. She leaned forward with her forearms pressed against her thighs. I sat on the sofa between them with my back to the window. Red, purple, and yellow flowers—the same as the ones outside—were in pots on either side of me. Three water bottles were placed on a glass table in the middle of the room.

"Where does it all start?" I asked. "Where did the idea of leaving Punjab come from?"

Massar Ji explained that he and his younger brother Harbhajan first heard of America when they were teenagers. Growing up, they were immersed in the culture of Punjab: they played field hockey and kabaddi, and acted in school plays based on the life of Bhagat Singh. The older they got though, the more they learned of the world around them. They read a book in high school called *America and Her People* that had pictures of American things like Cadillac cars and the landscapes of Alaska. They told themselves they would drive that car and visit that place one day. They came from a poor farming family in Punjab and, just like Dad, they were plunged deep into debt with the introduction of The Green Revolution in the sixties.

"There was no future in India," Massar Ji said. He rested his hands in his lap. I wasn't expecting his answer to be so simple, so hopeless. "I graduated from Punjab University in the sixties and worked as a machinist," he continued. "I operated a metalworking lathe at a factory during the days and taught classes at the university in the evenings. Our family was poor though. I could have stayed working as a machinist making 200 rupees a month, or as a teacher making anywhere from 100 to 300 rupees a month, but there wasn't any opportunity in that." He looked past me and stared out the window. "Not for the level of poverty we were in."

Massar Ji detailed how he had used the money he earned from his metalworking and teaching jobs to construct several roads and a sewer system in his village of Dhilwan, but he wasn't earning enough cash to bring about the type of change he wanted to see for the community.

"My parents had neighbours and friends around that time who sent their kids to work in the UK," he explained. "One British pound was worth a lot of rupees back then. People who started with five acres of land now had over a hundred acres after their children went away to Europe. The rest of us in the village only saw the results of the work. We had no idea what work people were actually doing once they left Punjab."

"So it was your parents' idea for you to leave?" I asked.

Massar Ji shook his head. "It was my idea. I saw how things were going and how stuck we were. Once I made up my mind, my parents supported me in whatever direction I wanted to go."

"If everyone else was going to England, how did you decide on Canada?"

"I had only ever heard the name of Canada. I really didn't know where or what it was," Massar Ji said. He smiled as he spoke. "I needed to make money and people told us Canada was where the money was. My plan was to come here for five or six years, save up, and go back home to Punjab."

"If the family didn't have much money, how did you travel?" Much like Dad's journey, it was the big questions of how and why that I was most curious about.

"I had to borrow the money."

Massar Ji and his parents had to turn to the same predatory system of private lenders that Dhadha Ji dealt with in the sixties. I didn't understand why so many people went to these loan sharks when the interest rates were so high, but that was a desperation I had never experienced before. I didn't know what it was like to live somewhere and feel that there was no other option but to escape.

"I tried to come to Canada twice in 1970," Massar Ji explained. "I first tried in March but the travel agent I paid to arrange my flight took my money and ran off with it. I never saw him again."

"How did you get out then?"

"I had to take out another loan. My parents told me not to worry about the money. They said if it's hukam for me to go to Canada, then I'll go." He stopped to reach for a water bottle, unscrewed the cap, and took a sip. "I eventually came to Canada in August of that year. The last thing my mom said to me before I left home was to look out for my older sister and to do whatever I could to bring her to Canada once I was able to get myself settled." Massar Ji's voice trembled. It was a slight quiver, but it stood out given how composed he always kept himself. The older sister that he spoke of was Dhadhi Ji. Whenever I saw them interact while she was still alive, Massar Ji always bowed his head and touched her feet when he greeted her as a show of respect.

"Did you need a visa or any kind of paperwork to travel?" I asked. I was curious to learn the details of the voyage. It was one thing for Massar Ji to be bold enough to dream, but it fascinated me that he had the ingenuity to figure things out for himself in a time before the internet or reliable access to phones.

Massar Ji explained that as two nations part of the British Commonwealth, citizens of India didn't need a visa to enter Canada at the time. Dad had also mentioned this loophole to me before. He told me how Indians back in the sixties and seventies would fly to Canada without needing any documentation other than a passport. Some of them used the opportunity to work for jobs that paid cash off the books and under the table. Travel agents in India were capitalizing on people's desires to earn money in the West to the point they sometimes booked entire chartered planes full of Indian nationals to send to Canada for the purposes of undocumented labour.

"I didn't have anywhere to go when I landed in Toronto, so I stayed at Pape Gurudwara," Massar Ji said.

The gurudwara at 269 Pape Avenue in Toronto was established in April 1969, just a year before Massar Ji had arrived. Prior to its opening, the small Sikh population in the city used to gather at community centres in the area for monthly kirtans and services, and sought to establish a more permanent home for themselves. The gurudwara on Pape was the first one in Ontario and it became a hub for Sikhs who regularly travelled there from all across the province to pray and engage in seva.

"It's a really hard life to come to Canada and try settling down when you don't have anyone to help you," Massar Ji continued. "The support I received from people who I didn't know and who didn't have to help me was so important in those early years."

Massar Ji shared that he had met a man who frequently attended Pape Gurudwara named KP who lived in Whitby, a small town east of Toronto. Originally a Sikh from Kenya, KP owned several properties and businesses back home that provided him with a bit more financial security in Canada than newer immigrants like Massar Ji had. After KP negotiated with his landlord an increase of forty dollars per month in rent to cover the cost of an extra tenant in the unit, KP and his wife welcomed Massar Ji into their home. KP opened his wallet as well, telling Massar Ji to take cash whenever he needed it.

"He didn't want anything from me," Massar Ji said, blinking back tears. "He just told me to pay him back whenever I got on my feet and was able to make money for myself. Even after I was settled though, he didn't take a dollar from me."

In addition to money and shelter, KP also provided Massar Ji with guidance in navigating the immigration system, and advised him to apply for landed immigrant status in Oshawa rather than in Toronto. In 1970, there were 31 000 applications submitted by people seeking immigrant status in Canada, a number that far exceeded the expectations of immigration officials and resulted in a backlog in the processing of those applications. Understanding that the claim could take up to a year to process in Toronto, the same claim would only take a few months to complete in Oshawa away from the big city. True to KP's word, Massar Ji was able to get landed immigrant status by December 1970.

"What was the first job you worked when you came to Toronto?" I asked. "You had a degree and taught at your college, so were you able to find anything in your field?"

"I passed a trades test and got my work permit," Massar Ji replied. Even though many Indians were working in Canada illegally, he still made every effort to obtain the necessary paperwork and do things by the book. "I applied anywhere I could, whether it was related to my field of study or not. Every employer told me the same thing: I needed Canadian work experience. Of course, I didn't have any at this point. So, as an immigrant, there was no way I could get hired. Some employers said they would only hire me if I cut my hair and shaved my beard."

In Sikhi, keeping one's hair was a way of recognizing, accepting, and honouring the physical form one was given. Massar Ji wore a dastaar and had a long beard for as long as I could remember. When he didn't have his beard knotted up, it flowed down to his navel. When I was younger, I had seen some pictures of him and Dad from their early days in Canada and Europe in the seventies and eighties. It was fun for me and my cousins to laugh at how different our fathers looked back then without facial hair or turbans. We joked that Massar Ji looked like the pro wrestler Ted DiBiase and Dad looked like Uncle Jesse from Full House. What we didn't know at the time was that they were forced to look that way, reduced by Western fears in order to survive in places that didn't accept them. Feeling he had no choice if he wanted to find work and earn money in Canada, Massar Ji cut his hair and got his first job in late 1970 working as a security guard at the Royal York Hotel in downtown Toronto. He earned $1.38 an hour.

"A few months later, I got a job at a factory in Mississauga that made truck parts," Massar Ji shared. "The work there was so busy, there was no time to even wipe your sweat." By this point, Massar Ji had left Whitby and moved back to Toronto closer to Pape Gurudwara where he rented an apartment with six other Punjabi immigrants. "The new job paid $2.38 an hour. I was so happy that I would be making a whole dollar more," he laughed.

At his new job, Massar Ji was paired with the only other person of colour in the factory, another Punjabi man who had started working there just one day earlier. The two of them were stationed at the busiest part of the factory where they had to remove and organize parts that came down a conveyor belt. Compared to the overt biases that Massar Ji faced from employers who demanded that he cut his hair in order to be hired for a job, this was a move that he considered to be more subtle in its prejudice; if he and his colleague weren't able to keep up with the pace, it would slow down the workflow and draw the ire of everyone else on the all-white staff. It was an intentional move by management to force the two of them to get fed up with the work and quit.

"I remember my first shift at that job," Massar Ji said. "It was 3:45 p.m. and I was supposed to finish at four. I was so happy that I made it to the end of the day. The foreman came around and I wanted to make a good impression on him so I started working faster. He waved at me to get my attention. He held up four fingers on each hand and walked away without saying anything. I was confused so I turned to my co-worker. He told me that meant we had to work four hours of overtime until 8:00 p.m."

The other Punjabi man had explained to Massar Ji that the last person he saw turn down the overtime hours was fired on the spot. The foreman later returned at a quarter to eight and, without a word, held up six fingers to signify that they were to be back at work at 6:00 a.m. the next day.

"The subways didn't start running until six in the morning back then," Massar Ji recalled, "so I had to take a bus from my apartment at Pape and Gerrard to get to Eglinton station, and then take another bus to get to Mississauga where the factory was. There was hardly any bus service in Mississauga so I would have to walk four kilometres from the bus stop to get to work. Even when there were two feet of snow on the ground, I still made that walk twice a day."

"What did you do after work and on the weekends?" I asked. There had to be more to his life back then than just the factory, I thought.

"There was no time to do anything. I worked from six in the morning until 8:00 p.m. from Monday to Friday, and from eight in the morning to 4:00 p.m. on weekends. By the time I got home on a weekday, it would be after ten at night. I would slap some peanut butter on a piece of bread before going to bed, and do the whole thing all over again the next day. When I was in Punjab..."

Massar Ji stopped himself. I felt like he wanted to say something more but he wasn't sure if he should.

"When I was in Punjab, I had only drank alcohol two or three times in my life. In Canada, the culture was different. Everyone would ask each other to go out for drinks after a shift. When I came home after work, I would have a few drinks to help me sleep. I needed something to get to bed quickly so I could go to work again in the morning. I would work, drink, and lie down. That was the cycle. I felt that if I needed to work this hard to get by, I might as well go home and work hard in Punjab instead."

Massi Ji stood up and smoothed out the front of her purple salwaar. She left the room and I listened to the soft thumps of her footsteps cross the tiled floors of the house towards the kitchen. A rush of water from the faucet poured into a metal teapot.

Massar Ji noted that he got his opportunity to go back home to Punjab a few months after he had started working at the factory in Mississauga. In June 1971, he received a letter from his father informing him that his mother had fallen ill and was being monitored at a hospital in Ludhiana. There was only one phone in his parents' village of Dhilwan, and telephone use had to be scheduled by villagers several days in advance. Massar Ji didn't have time to waste. He booked himself on the earliest flight he could find to be with his ailing mother in Punjab. When he had made it home to Dhilwan, he was greeted by his Massi.

"She was surprised to see me," Massar Ji said. He spoke slowly, like it hurt him for each word to leave his chest. "I asked her how my mom was doing. My Massi was quiet. There was a long pause before she said, 'Beta, did nobody tell you? The funeral is already over.'"

I tried to picture the exhaustion Massar Ji must have experienced that day flying from Toronto to Delhi, and then travelling the eight-hour trek from Delhi to Dhilwan. I tried to picture the panic in his eyes as he looked around the house for someone who could give him some answers and take him to the hospital to see his mother. I imagined the way his heart must have pounded against his ribcage as if it was trying to break through the bars and escape. I tried to place myself in the confusion his Massi must have felt, first at seeing her nephew without his beard and dastaar, unrecognizable from the man he was when he left home less than a year ago, and then to see him home unannounced. I tried to imagine the silence between them before she told him it was too late, how her quiet must have communicated more than any words ever could have. I tried to picture the tears, the wails, the buckling knees, the trembling chests, the hugs, the grief. I thought about Mom.

Massar Ji wiped a tear from his eye before it could fall. He inhaled deeply and collected his composure. "People in the village asked me more about why I was back in Punjab than they did about my mother," he said. "They asked me if I got deported or if I'd given up on making it in Canada."

As much as Massar Ji had thought about leaving Toronto behind and returning to Punjab permanently, he remembered the promise he made to his mother that he would help the family and look out for his sister. He wasn't about to go back on his word now.

Upon his return to Toronto in the summer of 1971, Massar Ji described that the working conditions in the factory were the least of his worries.

As migration from different parts of South Asia to Toronto increased, so too did racial tensions.

"It wasn't just employers being racist to us behind closed doors," he said. "I would see 'Paki' or 'go home' written on houses and businesses that our people owned. People who looked like me were getting beaten up in the streets. A lot of Indians formed gangs for self-defence against the white buggers who were beating us up. I knew people who kept cricket bats in their trunks in case they got attacked. We fought them in the courts too."

Massar Ji explained that when he volunteered as a secretary at Pape Gurudwara, a Sikh man came in who was being denied a job with the Toronto Transit Commission. He was told to cut his hair and shave his beard if he wanted to be a streetcar driver, and he asked if the gurudwara could give him a letter that explained the importance of hair in Sikhi and why he couldn't be asked to cut his.

"We took his case to the Ontario Labour Board and won," Massar Ji said. "It was the first time a Sikh had won a case like that in Ontario." He smiled as he reflected on his accomplishment, his cheeks tinged a familiar shade of rosy pink.

Massi Ji returned to the room and balanced three white teacups atop a wooden serving tray. Swirls of steam rose up from the cups. She set the tray down on the table, took a cup, and sat back on the ottoman.

In 1971 and '72, Massar Ji supported his brothers Nirmolak and Harbhajan in moving from Punjab to Toronto. As we drank our tea, I thought about how Massar Ji fought for himself and for the people he belonged to. It was through his struggle that people who look like me became normalized in this part of the world. Massar Ji paid it forward for us the same way KP did for him.

I also thought about how much things hadn't changed since 1970. Living in Malton for the first eleven years of my life, all my friends were from South Asia and the Caribbean. When we moved to Brampton in 1998 though, that all changed. I didn't see the same faces I grew up with. I heard racial epithets from white classmates daily, sometimes from kids who said the words so often that they didn't know they were using slurs, privileged enough to be oblivious to consequence. Other times, the words were used against me with all the intention of a sharpened prison shank. Sometimes people hurled curses out their car windows when they drove by me and Dad as we worked in the front yard.

My patka, and later my dastaar, were host to the unwelcome hands of classmates, teachers, and airport security guards who all poked and grabbed at my head without asking. *Go back to where you came from. You don't belong here. This isn't your country. You should be thankful that we even allowed your people in. Take that towel off your head. We speak English here.* I'd heard them all, time and time again. It was exhausting that I wasn't allowed to just be, that I had to constantly explain and defend myself. Some days, I felt that it would have been easier not to fight back, and just let the hate wash over me. I wondered how Massar Ji had the bravery not to give in.

***

In the days after my talk with Massar Ji, I thought a lot about race and how it was discussed in Canada. In a speech at the World Economic Forum in 2016, Canadian Prime Minister Justin Trudeau famously called diversity a source of strength. In social studies classes I took in middle school, teachers spoke proudly of Canada's role in helping enslaved people escape the United States; no mention was ever made though of how Canadian settlers also enslaved Black and Indigenous people for two centuries. When matters of race hit the national conscience, the pervading commentary tended to be that no matter how bad things were in Canada, at least we weren't as bad as the Americans. There was very little critical reflection in Canadian media of our history with racism, and how racism still impacted modern times.

Though Massar Ji was proud of the fact that he was able to help one Sikh man win a case at the Ontario Labour Board, I reflected on a few recent acts of violence that showed me our country was still far from equitable. In 2016, a coroner's inquest into the fatal police shooting of Jermaine Carby was released. The investigation into the incident, which had originally taken place in Brampton in 2014, sought to understand why Jermaine—a Black man—was asked by police to provide his identification when he was just a passenger in a car that had been pulled over for a traffic stop. The officer who fired the fatal shots admitted that he had only interacted with Jermaine for the purposes of completing a street check, which is the process of questioning an individual and documenting their personal information even though no crime is being committed or investigated. Analyses of street check data in Toronto have shown that this policy discriminately targets Black people. The coroner's inquest stated that unconscious bias and racial profiling played a role in Jermaine's shooting, and that these issues needed to be better addressed in the police force.

Also in 2016, an Indigenous man named Colten Boushie was shot in the head at point blank range in rural Saskatchewan after an altercation with a white farmer. In each respective case, Black and Indigenous activists and community leaders called out and confronted Canada's legacy of racism. As Sikhs, we hadn't been in this country all that long in comparison, but we were still subject to that legacy all the same. I found that there was so much we could learn from the strength shown by our Black and Indigenous counterparts; whenever justice was denied, they continued to make their voices heard again and again. Massar Ji showed me that for our community to survive here, we had to be willing to show up and speak out for ourselves and for others.

SCHOOLING & EDUCATION

Satnam parked the tractor by the side of the dirt road and killed the engine. He was nineteen years old. His sweat glued the back of his shirt to the tractor's black leather seat. The smells of fertilizer and exhaust fumes singed his nostrils.

Satnam's Mamma Ji—Sampuran's brother Gurmukh—and the other farm labourers exited from a square trolley hooked to the back of the tractor. After Gurmukh had seen all three of his brothers leave Punjab for Toronto, he needed help running his farm in Dhilwan. Satnam's younger brothers Mohinder and Sardara were growing up; Sampuran gave them more responsibility on the farm in Nawan Pind, and arranged for Satnam to live and work with Gurmukh. Dhilwan was closer to DAV College in Jalandhar where Satnam was studying economics, English, and political science, so moving there also allowed him to save time on his commute to class every day.

It was late in the afternoon and the sun was still fierce. The workers who joined Satnam and Gurmukh were women from Dhilwan and other nearby villages. They all scattered themselves throughout the field and squatted in the damp, orange-brown soil lined with rows of green plumage that belonged to peanut plants ready to be harvested.

After several hours of removing the plants from the earth and shaking the dirt off their roots, Gurmukh motioned towards the tractor.

"It'll be dark soon," he said to Satnam. "Let's wrap this up."

Satnam jogged over to the trolley to retrieve several white sheets and brought them out to the peanut field. He unfolded each sheet and laid them flat on the soil. Each woman piled her haul of peanut plants atop a sheet of fabric, tied the corners of the fabric together, hoisted the bindle atop her head, and walked back to the trolley.

The red sun had nearly completed its descent under the horizon. Satnam tried starting the tractor. The engine grumbled and sputtered before going silent. He turned the key again. The engine moaned but didn't start.

"Mamma Ji, what do I do?" Satnam asked.

Gurmukh exited the trolley and walked around to the front of the tractor. Satnam joined him and they looked under the hood together.

"Everything looks alright to me," Gurmukh said. Satnam squinted, struggling to see the engine's components under the last embers of sunlight. He tried starting the tractor once more, but the engine refused.

"It's still early," Gurmukh said, scratching his head through his mint green dastaar. "Someone in the village should still be awake. I'll walk back and see if I can get them to tow us. You all wait here." Gurmukh exited the trolley and headed home. The sound of the dirt crunching under his feet interrupted the growing chorus of crickets chirping.

Twenty minutes later, Gurmukh returned on a tractor driven by Deepa, a man in his early sixties who lived just a few houses down from Gurmukh. Deepa was dressed in an orange dastaar and a light grey kurtha with the sleeves rolled up to his elbows. He parked in front of Satnam and secured the two tractors together using a length of rope.

"All set! Let's go," Deepa said. He climbed back aboard his tractor and pressed down on the gas pedal, pulling forward the inoperative tractor manned by Satnam, and the trolley occupied by Gurmukh and the other workers.

As their procession rumbled forward, Deepa struggled to get his tractor up an incline in the road. Despite the darkness of the evening, Satnam recognized the hill they were on, and he knew that there were train tracks that passed across the top of it. Deepa pressed down harder on the gas pedal. Satnam looked to the right of the hill. Through the silhouettes of the trees lining the tracks, he saw the lights of a train approaching in the distance.

"Hey, slow down!" Satnam yelled. He waited for Deepa to turn around or to show some sign that he had heard the warning over the sound of the tractor's engine. The hill didn't have any signs or crossing signals to warn pedestrians and drivers of oncoming trains.

"Stop! Please, stop!" Gurmukh and the labourers joined Satnam in calling out to get Deepa's attention. Satnam stomped on his tractor's brake pedal to try to slow the convoy down but Deepa continued inching the caravan forward. Deepa made it over the hump to reach the top of the hill at the same time the oncoming train slammed through his tractor.

The cries of the women in the trolley were drowned out by the screams of steel being ripped apart. Satnam and Gurmukh leapt out of their seats to see if Deepa was still alive. The wind from the still-passing train caused dirt from the road to rise. Red clouds of dust trembled in the yellow light that bled out of the windows of the train cars speeding by. The front half of Deepa's tractor was torn completely off; the disembodied back wheels still stood beside the train tracks. Satnam and Gurmukh couldn't find Deepa's body.

Satnam walked parallel to the tracks and followed the direction of the train. From the shrubs below, he heard a voice.

"Hello?"

It was Deepa. He sounded calm. Satnam called over to Gurmukh and the two of them followed Deepa's voice.

"I need some help getting up," Deepa laughed. "I'm trying to stand but I can't seem to put any weight on my right leg."

In the moonlight, Satnam looked down at Deepa's leg. It had been severed at the knee. A few strands of skin and sinew hung from his thigh. A stream of blood poured from his leg, soaked through his clothes, and formed an expanding puddle of crimson beneath him. Satnam looked at Gurmukh and shook his head, silently communicating to his uncle not to draw attention to Deepa's injury; they didn't want Deepa to panic.

The sound of quickening footsteps over crushed gravel approached. "What do you think you're doing?" a man's voice said. "I've got two hundred people on that train. You could have killed us all with that stunt you were trying to pull!"

In the darkness, Satnam couldn't make out what the man looked like, just that he had a cap and uniform on. The train conductor, he assumed.

"This guy's tractor engine is stuck under my train so now I can't do my job," the conductor continued. "I've got deadlines and—"

"We're sorry, but we've got to get him to a hospital now," Gurmukh said.

"A hospital? I don't think so." The conductor bent over, hooked his hands under Deepa's armpits and dragged him towards the back of the halted train.

"You're acting crazy," Gurmukh shouted, chasing behind the conductor.

The conductor lifted Deepa's body onto the caboose. "He's not going anywhere. He's messing with my money. I'm calling the police and having him arrested. Either that or I'll have him pay me back for the damages."

"Arrested? What good is arresting him if he's dead?" Gurmukh yelled.

The conductor reached out with both hands to shove Gurmukh away. Satnam pulled his uncle back before they could make contact.

"Just look at him," Satnam said.

The conductor adjusted his cap and looked over at Deepa. The lower half of his body dangled over the rust-brown edge of the caboose. Blood poured from his amputated leg like a waterfall to the gravel below.

"Let us take him to the hospital," Satnam said. "Please."

Gurmukh took off, walking away from the train back towards the dirt road where his tractor and trolley were still parked.

"Hey, where are you going?" the conductor demanded.

"To the next village," Gurmukh called over his shoulder. "I know a guy with a car. I'll have him drive us to the hospital. I'm not letting Deepa die on my watch."

Ten minutes later, headlights pierced through the dark. Gurmukh and a nearby villager returned in a car and drove alongside the train tracks to where Deepa, Satnam, and the conductor waited. Satnam had torn a piece of fabric off his sleeve and tied it around Deepa's thigh to try and stop the bleeding. Satnam and the other villager carried Deepa into the backseat of the car. Gurmukh climbed into the passenger seat. The driver sped off towards the main road. Satnam watched as the headlights pulled away from the conductor and the blood-soaked train.

***

When I graduated from McMaster University in the spring of 2008, I didn't plan on attending my convocation. I was looking ahead to a fresh start at grad school in the fall and wanted a clean break from my time as an undergraduate. My parents urged me to attend my graduation though.

Academically, I performed well in high school, averaging high Bs and low As. I excelled in sciences like chemistry and biology, but I struggled in my first few years at university. The combination of a heavy workload and a lengthy commute made it difficult to find enough time to devote to each of my classes. Despite my floundering grades, Dad tried his best to put me in every position to succeed. He didn't want me to work a job during the semesters so that I could focus all of my attention on my studies. When I struggled with calculus in my first year, he sought out a private tutor to help me understand the concepts better. When I was delayed in my commute on the bus due to traffic, or if I came home at midnight after a night class, Dad suggested that I rent an apartment close to campus. I told him that I was okay at home and could manage. I was grateful and privileged that my parents supported my schooling the way they did, but I also felt guilty for going to university in the first place. I felt it was my fault that this large financial strain was being placed on the family, and my poor grades made me feel like a burden to my parents.

Whenever I asked Dad how he could afford for me to go to school, he told me not to worry about money. To my parents, education was a trusted and safe pathway to success in Canada. In their eyes, it was the order that the system in the West was built upon, and all I had to do was follow the ladder up. From their perspective, education was the key to unlocking financial stability, a seat at the table, and freedom to choose, pursue, and prosper—all the things that the instability of immigration and manual labour jobs didn't allow my parents to have for themselves. I felt that was a lot of pressure to live up to. I internalized the weight of their expectations and told myself that it was on me to deliver on the promise of what they were told Canada could offer, that I had to become something that justified everything they gave up in Punjab to get here, and that I had to bear the sum of their sacrifices and prove that it wasn't all for nothing. In the end, I decided to attend my graduation for my parents' sake. It meant a lot for them to see me walk across the stage and get my degree.

"How did you do in school?" I asked Dad.

We were eating dinner together at the kitchen table. Roti with saag. Relatives regularly brought over food for us while Mom was in the hospital. They figured we already had enough to worry about that we didn't also need to fret about preparing meals. Our fridge was stocked with margarine and takeout containers that were repurposed and full of different homemade dhaals, sabjis, and comfort foods.

Dad was waiting for his night shift with Mom at the hospital to start. Since the surgery, Dad hadn't been sleeping much. He would get home from Sunnybrook in the mornings after someone came to relieve him, but he typically only ended up sleeping until noon. He would try to fall back asleep a few hours later, but he said the sunlight leaking through the blinds kept him awake.

"I liked studying the sciences in high school," Dad explained. A stack of rotis wrapped in aluminum foil sat on top of a pile of newspapers. "I did my homework and helped on the farm every day and still managed to get good grades. The older I got though, the more my classmates and relatives pushed me towards things like economics and English—stuff that would help me make money and find work away from home. I was a good student, but it was a big adjustment going to college. On top of my classes, I had moved from Nawan Pind to Dhilwan and worked with Gurmukh Mamma Ji there on his farm." Dad paused to swallow a bite and washed it down with a sip of water from a steel cup. "I ended up failing my last year in college and had to repeat it."

"You failed a year?" I leaned back in my seat. I couldn't stop the slight smile curling on my lips.

Dad pushed me hard to succeed in school for as long as I could remember. I dreaded bringing home a mark less than a B+. He always demanded better of me. When I was in elementary school, he assigned me homework from math books he had shipped to us from Punjab. In my classes in Canada, I hadn't yet covered the concepts he was asking me to work through. The equations looked like a different language to me. He would just tell me to study harder until I figured it out. I would be in tears trying to solve the questions, wondering why I wasn't smart enough for him. Learning now that Dad failed and had to repeat a year, but I had to perform at the highest level, made me laugh to myself at the irony.

"I was doing so much on the farm there in Dhilwan," Dad explained. "Most of my uncles were in Canada by then, so I had to step up and take on a lot of the work. I didn't have the time to study. It took me four years to do a three-year program, but I still got my B.A. in economics."

It made sense now why Dad didn't want me to work a job and attend classes at the same time while I was in university: in his eyes, too much was riding on my achievement. He didn't perceive his time in college as having the same value as a Western education.

"The expectation was different for me," Dad continued. He scraped the sides of the bowl with his spoon to sweep up the last earthy green streaks of saag. "I wasn't meant to stay in Punjab and use my education there. We couldn't keep relying on farming. We couldn't keep doing the same work we had always done. We were in too much debt for that. I had to do something to change the situation. Seeing people around me leave for England and Canada showed me that I would have to leave the village too."

"How did you decide on Greece then? Why not Canada where your uncles were?" I asked. Though I didn't know many details about Dad's journey from Punjab to Canada, he had mentioned to me in the past that he spent several years working aboard a Greek cargo ship. I didn't know how he got there though.

"The Canadian immigration laws changed while I was still in college," Dad shared, filling in some of the gaps. "My uncles flew directly from India to Toronto without needing visas, but I couldn't do that. The new law was that you had to apply within India to get a visa to visit Canada. I would have been denied though, so I didn't bother applying."

"Why would they deny you?"

"Think about it. I was young, poor, unmarried, and had no work experience. If I applied for a visitor visa to Canada, the Indian government would have assumed I was only going there to try to make money and work illegally. And if I applied for a work visa, I would have had to show what work I was qualified for, and that there was a demand for my skills in the Canadian labour market. At that point, the only job I had ever done was on the farm."

Dad explained that he had heard from classmates and people in other villages that the port city of Piraeus in Greece was home to the head offices of many shipping companies that sent cargo ships out to deliver goods internationally. Crews on each ship could be as large as twenty-five to forty men, so jobs were abundant if one could somehow make their way to Greece. Dad had never been on a ship before—he didn't even know how to swim—and he didn't know anyone who had personally travelled from India to Greece to work on a ship, but that was the destination he had chosen for himself.

"We didn't know for sure if people were telling the truth or not about

Greece," Dad noted, "but if you hear the same thing from enough places, you start to take notice."

"That was all it took?" My eyes were wide, eyebrows raised.

"We were pressed to the point that we just had to follow where we thought the opportunity was," he shrugged. That was all it took.

Dad said that for people who made it to Greece, working on a ship was safer than any other job that paid workers under the table. The shipping companies in Greece didn't ask to see if a worker was granted a visa by their home nation; one could be hired there even without having their paperwork in order. For every crewmate that was under a shipping company's employ, the company would handle the visas and paperwork for each worker on the team so that they could legally enter every international destination they delivered cargo to. This allowed them the safety to load, unload, and refuel in any country without worrying about the status of their documentation.

"That makes sense," I nodded to myself. "But why did you have to leave India entirely? Couldn't you find work in another part of the country?"

Dad shook his head. "We had no solution for the floods, but we couldn't pack up and leave Nawan Pind either because there was nowhere else to go. We would still have to buy land and build a new home no matter where we went. We didn't have the money for that, so we stayed where we were. That was the nature of farming. We couldn't be happy when we had a good harvest and then turn around and be sad when we had droughts or floods. We had to work with what the earth gave us. There was no large-scale industry in Punjab other than farming, and we weren't close to any seaports, so we didn't have many job opportunities. Some people worked in government jobs or as teachers, but other than farming and the military, there wasn't much to do in Punjab. The Indian government was scared to put any industry there because we were right by the border with Pakistan."

After partition in 1947, Indian Prime Minister Jawaharlal Nehru believed that political and economic independence for a free India could only come through industrialization and resource development. Mining of coal and iron increased after the British left, and new steel plants were constructed in eastern Indian regions such as Rourkela, Bhilai and Durgapur throughout the fifties and sixties. However, during this time period, new industries weren't being introduced in Punjab. Industrial units constructed there after partition only aided in farming activities like grain processing, leaving Punjab to fulfill a very specific role within India's industrial landscape. Mounting debts accrued under private lenders and the middleman system left Dad with few options. Seeking opportunities abroad became his best choice if he wanted to change the family's fortunes.

"So, you decided to go to Greece instead of Canada because you didn't need a visa to get there?" I tried to connect some of the dots.

"No, it was the same in Greece as it was in Canada," Dad said. "The Indian government was becoming aware that people were using visitor visas to go to Greece and find work, so they made it harder for people to travel there too."

"Then how did you get to Greece if you couldn't get a visa?"

"We found ways," Dad said. He averted his gaze from mine. He stacked his empty bowl on top of his plate. "Canada was across the ocean from Punjab. Greece wasn't as far. We found people to help us get there."

***

The human smugglers who led people out of Punjab in search of work and economic prosperity in Europe often hid in plain sight. Satnam walked into a travel agency in Jalandhar, its storefront just as ordinary and unremarkable as the other shops alongside it. He was twenty years old. Satnam's childhood friend Boota was the one who had set up this meeting. Satnam didn't know much about the man he was going to meet, only that he worked as a travel agent and went by the nickname of The Coyote. His office at the travel agency doubled as his headquarters where he spoke with potential clients who sought access to the West to find jobs and opportunity.

The Coyote's office inside was just as nondescript as its exterior: all four walls of the square room were covered in wood panelling. A single light bulb hung from exposed wiring in the centre of the room. Reliable access to electricity was only a few years old in this part of Punjab. A green, metal cabinet stood in the corner to the left of a heavy, wooden desk. A world map was taped to the wall behind an office chair. A thin grey carpet that had become weathered under footsteps covered the floor. Satnam looked at the cabinet. One of the drawers was half open and brimming with manila folders. Past clients, he presumed.

"So, what can I do for you?" The Coyote asked. He was clad in a white dress shirt tucked into brown slacks. "I need your help to get to Europe," Satnam said. "I want to work to make some money for my family. I heard the shipping industry in Greece is huge. I was told you can help me get there."

A smirk slithered across The Coyote's face. "Greece, huh? Oh, that's really far. A young guy like you wants to go all the way out there?"

"Yes," Satnam responded, unsure if his patchy beard was hiding the heat and redness he felt in his cheeks.

A few months before Satnam had asked Boota to arrange this meeting with The Coyote, Bachittar returned from Toronto to Punjab to get married. During their talks, Bachittar brought Satnam up to speed on what his life in Canada was like—the work, the sweat, the isolation, the money. Bachittar figured Greece would be the same.

The Coyote leaned forward, placed his elbows on the desk and laced his fingers in front of him. "Listen, I've been doing this a long time," he said. "Do you think it's easy to go to Greece? It's not easy, you understand? It takes a lot of money. A lot of risk. Do you have money? And if you don't, where are you going to get it from?" The Coyote's restless leg and the sound of his slipper repeatedly slapping his heel matched the pace of Satnam's heartbeat.

"I can get money," said Satnam, trying his best to maintain a poker face.

"Okay, listen...it's not exactly a direct flight to Athens but here's how it goes. I'll get you a tourist visa from Delhi so you can fly from Amritsar to Kabul." The Coyote stood up and pushed his chair aside. He pointed to where Afghanistan was on the map behind him. Satnam followed where The Coyote's fingers moved. "Once we're in Kabul, we'll go to the Iranian embassy there and apply for a tourist visa. We travel by bus from Kabul to Tehran. When we get to Iran, we apply for a tourist visa to Turkey from the embassy there. And we do this, country by country, until we make our way to Greece." The Coyote sat down again and leaned back in his chair. "Like I said, this takes money. I need twelve thousand rupees up front before I do any work on my end. I'm not putting myself on the line for you unless I know you're all the way in."

Satnam was expressionless. He looked down at his shoes where he felt his heart sink. He didn't have that kind of money. He didn't even have a passport. He glanced over at the cabinet again and wondered how the names on those folders sat in this same chair and decided their fates. Greece suddenly seemed a lot further than it did on The Coyote's map.

"Why don't I give you some time to think about it, huh?" The Coyote muttered. He rose from his chair to signify the meeting was over. "You know where to find me."

The Coyote escorted Satnam from the dim lighting of his office into the sunshine and busy market outside. Cyclists whizzed by. Voices chattered and laughed and bartered over the price of goods. Before leaving the travel agency, Satnam paused and leaned against the doorframe for stability, his vision temporarily blinded by the brightness of the world before him.

***

On March 13, 1974, just before graduating from college, Satnam received his first ever passport from the Regional Passport Office in Chandigarh. Satnam gathered most of the twelve thousand rupees he needed to facilitate his travels through private lenders. As a sign of appreciation for the work Satnam did on the farm in Dhilwan while attending college, Gurmukh Mamma Ji also contributed what money he could.

As part of the deal to get to Greece, Satnam surrendered both his passport and his money to The Coyote up front. On Satnam's behalf, The Coyote applied for a tourist visa to Afghanistan and arranged for Satnam to fly from Raja Sansi Aerodrome in Amritsar to Kabul on August 6, 1975. The Coyote explained that Satnam would be accompanied on this journey by twelve other men who also sought entry into Greece. As part of the deal, there was a two-week window by which all thirteen of The Coyote's clients needed to arrive at the designated motel in Kabul. If any of them were unable to make it there by the established deadline, the group would leave for Tehran without them, and without returning the money that was paid.

***

Satnam walked across the sizzling tarmac to where his plane awaited him. He was twenty-one years old. He ascended up the stairs and ducked his head to enter the aircraft. At least there's air conditioning in here, he thought. He followed the number printed on his ticket to find his seat.

From where Satnam sat in the middle of the plane, he could see all the way to the front and back of the aircraft. The plane wasn't full. He noticed a few other Sikh men aboard who appeared similar in age to him. He wondered if they were travelling for the same reasons he was and how they said goodbye to their families. Satnam replayed his own goodbyes in his head. Back in Nawan Pind, Sampuran pulled him in for hugs and buried her face in his chest, her tears leaving dark, damp spots on his shirt. Satnam cried too. Sampuran told him to be safe and to send letters whenever he could. Dhanna accompanied Satnam on the train ride from the village to the airport. Dhanna told Satnam not to be afraid; they didn't say much to each other aside from that. Satnam was dropped off outside the airport and had to figure out the rest of the journey on his own. He had never been this far away from home before. Satnam was shaken from his memories when the pilot said something over the intercom, though he couldn't make out what the message was. Scrambled static.

The plane moved forward, wheels shaking off their slumber. Taxiing into position for takeoff, Satnam felt the whir of the jet engines reverberate through his ribs. The plane gathered momentum and the gravity sunk him deeper into his seat. He swallowed saliva to try to stabilize the pressure in his ears. He repeated his father's words to himself—don't be afraid. Satnam looked out the window. Buildings shrunk in size the higher up the plane went. Acres of farmland became atoms that Satnam could let slip through his fingers. The clouds blocked the world below from his view. When he saw land again, he would be in a different country. Satnam quietly smiled to himself at the prospects of a new beginning. Maybe this risk would pay off. Maybe things would turn out okay. Maybe this would all be worth it.

SEVEN

CHAPTER • 09

DOLLARS

One of the few times I heard my family openly discuss their past in Punjab was around 2009. Dad explained that there had been a death in the family. Gulzar Singh, my Dhadhi's Chacha—my grandmother's uncle—had died in Punjab. Nobody knew how old he was. I knew few details of my grandparents' generation; I knew nothing of the generations that stretched further back in time.

Dad told me that one of Gulzar's brothers served with the British army and had been stationed in Iraq during World War I. Gulzar was in the British army as well. A story that Dad and Bachittar Massar Ji shared with pride after Gulzar's death was from World War II when Gulzar's relationship with the military came to a point of contention at the intersection of his loyalties to his uniform and his faith.

As part of the team that would operate field artillery, Gulzar was ordered by the British to exchange his dastaar for a helmet. Gulzar was defiant and argued that Sikhs had fought with the British military for decades without having to wear a helmet. He threatened to go on a hunger strike if the army wouldn't allow him to fight with the symbols of this faith intact, but he was court-martialed and sentenced to spend seven years in a Hong Kong prison.

The family in Punjab didn't know Gulzar had been jailed—the British military didn't ever contact them to let them know what had happened. As the war ended and the years went on, the family assumed Gulzar had died in combat, until one day he returned to the village every bit as alive as the day he was deployed. His resolve to put his faith before himself, to be unbent by Western standards, was something Dad and Massar Ji admired. Those battles between identity and assimilation also came to a head during my father's journey to Europe.

***

Satnam arrived in Kabul after a ninety-minute flight. Some of the other men on the plane who boarded with him in Amritsar were also part of The Coyote's group that would be travelling to Greece. One of them was Harjinder, a slender and tall man with a beard that hung down to his belt buckle. He was in his late twenties, owned a small restaurant in Jalandhar, and was a newlywed. The others were Paramjit and Kewal, a pair of short and stocky cousins with clean-shaven faces. Both from farming families, Paramjit and Kewal had seen their parents suffer through debts after dealing with loan sharks, which made their small-time farms less feasible as career paths. Satnam, Harjinder, Paramjit and Kewal all bunked in a room together as they waited for the other nine men from their troupe to make it to the motel.

The Coyote was the last one to arrive, landing closer to the end of the two-week window. Nobody could get in much of a word with him. He spent his first few days in Kabul in seclusion and made calls from the phone in his motel room. When he emerged, he told his clients that plans had changed—Greece was no longer on the table. The Coyote explained that he had spoken to a few of his contacts and they informed him that the Greek government wasn't giving visas to anyone due to ongoing political issues in the country.

In 1973, two years before The Coyote arranged this expedition for Satnam and the other twelve clients, the Organization of Arab Petroleum Exporting Countries instated an oil embargo against nations they perceived to be supportive of Israel during the Yom Kippur War. The embargo led to an immediate surge in oil prices and a spike in the rate of inflation which damaged the Greek economy. The fallout of that oil crisis saw a reduction in the number of visas being granted to people seeking entry into Greece. The Coyote said that Italy was now the new destination. He reassured his clients that the shipping industry there was just as big as it was in Greece.

On August 16, 1975, all thirteen men were granted visitor visas from the Iranian embassy in Kabul. Later that same day, they were also granted visas by the Italian embassy in Afghanistan. At both embassies, Satnam walked through the backstory just as The Coyote had instructed him, explaining that he had recently graduated from college and was sightseeing through the Middle East and Europe with friends as a reward to himself.

In Tehran, The Coyote held the door of his hotel room open and he asked Satnam, Harjinder, and one of the other members of their group to come inside. The three of them sat on the bed with Satnam positioned in the middle. The bed was parallel to the window and the blinds were turned halfway down. Grey light from the overcast sky fell on their backs.

"There's no easy way to say this," The Coyote said, pacing around the room. The space between his words was filled by the sound of his shoes shuffling against the tiles of the hotel room floor. "We're leaving Iran tomorrow for Turkey. That's Europe. Out there, there aren't a lot of people that look like you three do."

Satnam looked to Harjinder on his left who sat by the foot of the bed, and the other man on his right near the headboard. Out of the thirteen men on this expedition to Italy, they were the only three who wore dastaars and kept their beards flowing and unshorn. Satnam opened his mouth to speak but was cut off by The Coyote before a sound escaped.

"Don't say anything yet," The Coyote said. "I need you to listen." He stopped pacing and placed his hands on his hips. "I'm the only out of all of you who's made this trip to Europe before. I know what it's like there, okay? They don't like when people who look like you are around. Your turbans and beards are extra attention that we don't need."

Harjinder raised his chin to speak. "I don't feel that you—"

"I don't need you to feel," The Coyote interrupted. "I need you to think. People out there haven't seen anyone that looks the way you guys do. You're different. That scares them. Nobody's going to hire you if they're afraid of you. With a group this big, we already look suspicious enough. The last thing we need is more eyes on us. For all of our safety, I need you to cut your hair and shave your beards. To blend in."

Satnam shifted in his seat. The Coyote looked to the floor.

"There's a barbershop not too far from the motel," The Coyote said in a lowered voice. "We can do it there."

"Can we have a moment?" asked Satnam.

"Yes, of course, take your time." The Coyote walked backwards towards the door. "I'll just be outside." The lock clicked behind him as he exited.

Satnam sighed. "What do we do?"

"I don't want to do it," the third man said with his arms crossed. "I'll go back home if I have to. I'm not cutting anything. My father, my mother, my grandparents, their parents—none of us have ever cut our hair." He slammed his fist against the wooden headboard.

"I get it," Harjinder responded. "Everyone in this room feels the same way. All of our families are the same."

"What gives this guy the right to tell us to what to do?" the other man said. His voice increased in volume and agitation. "He's not a Sikh, he doesn't know—"

"Can you really go back home?" Satnam asked, disrupting their crossfire.

"What?" the other man said, his face contorted in anger.

"Can you really go back home?" Satnam repeated himself. "After all the money you borrowed to come on this trip, can you go back—can any of us go back—to our parents right now, empty handed and in more debt than we left them with?"

Harjinder and the other man both looked at Satnam. Neither of them said a word.

"I don't want to do this," Satnam continued. "I'm scared just like the both of you are. But we're in this now, and I understand why he's asking this of us. My uncle went to Toronto a few years ago and they did the same thing to him. He couldn't find work anywhere until he cut his hair."

"Italy is still so far away," Harjinder nodded. "We're not even halfway there yet. I can't afford to go back home. Not yet, anyway. My wife's depending on me. If it's safer for us to travel that way, then I think we should do it."

"Do you hear yourselves?" the other man pleaded. He stood up and started towards the door. Satnam grabbed him by his sleeve. "I can't go back home," the man said. Tears poured from the corners of his eyes.

"This isn't easy for us either," Satnam said. He let go of the man's wrist.

"We're in this together," Harjinder added. "We'll be right beside you when it happens."

Satnam opened the door and found The Coyote standing across

84

the hallway. Satnam didn't say a word, but the look on his face let The Coyote know that they were willing to move forward with his plan.

***

Dad's passport was difficult for me to follow. There were stamps in different languages from different embassies, and stamps placed on top of other stamps. Some of them had faded over time, others had letters that were thick and inky with letters that bled into each other. Few of them followed a chronological order.

"What part are you confused about?" Dad asked me.

"All of it," I said.

We sat cross-legged next to each other on the floor in what we called the paat room, or the prayer room. Dad started and ended every day in this room, meditating, praying. To our left were two floor-to-ceiling white bookshelves lined with rows of different texts, some in English, some in Punjabi, some filled with Gurbani, others written by scholars interpreting Gurbani. A black metallic fireplace sat flush against the wall between the bookshelves. Over the fireplace was a mantle with paintings of Guru Nanak Dev Ji and Guru Gobind Singh Ji. A small brown ceramic tile with prayer hands and white letters leaned on the mantle and stated 'the family that prays together, stays together.' Dad had a grey shawl spread across his lap and his reading glasses on. The rose gold-coloured arms of his specs were tucked into his orange parnaa. He always seemed more at peace when he was in this room. When he had a day off work, he spent hours at a time in here reading. Whatever stress he faced at work or with family, he didn't carry it into the paat room with him.

Mom had returned home from hospital just a few days prior. She spent eleven days at Sunnybrook after her surgery, and had a few minor scares with her breathing similar to the one Vijay and I had witnessed, but nothing too serious. By the end of her stay, Mom was walking the halls of the cancer ward for ten minutes at a time, sliding the bright green tennis balls on the legs of her walker to the end of the hall and looping back to her room. The staff at Sunnybrook were encouraged by her strength and progress. The family and medical staff felt Mom would be better able to continue her recovery at home where she could get back into some semblance of a routine. At the very least, she could sleep in her own bed again. Since returning home though, Mom wasn't sleeping much—she was still in too much pain from the surgery. As Dad and I sat in the paat room, Mom had finally managed to doze off upstairs. We tried to keep our voices down to let Mom hold on to what precious moments of slumber she could.

Dad held his passport open like a storybook. The faded, mint green pages were watermarked with the spinning wheel from India's flag. A purple stamp listed all the countries Dad was eligible to travel to.

Dad told me that the bigger stamps were from embassies that he had to physically walk into, like in Kabul, Tehran, and Istanbul. He and The Coyote's other clients travelled between those cities by coach bus and stayed in each place for a couple of days before moving to the next country. Five or six men slept together in a hotel room to save money. When they were on the road, they only stopped to refuel.

"What were those countries like?" I asked.

"I don't really remember," Dad said. "On the bus, everything started to look the same after a while. It was hard to keep track of where we were exactly. We travelled mostly on country roads and saw lots of farms. I remember Kabul being beautiful with all the mountains. It felt like a more advanced version of Jalandhar. In Tehran, they had posters of the shah everywhere. That's all that I can really remember."

I thought to myself what it meant for Dad to forget—or to supress—the sights of entire countries from his mind, to have lived through experiences that now felt more like hallucinations than they did memories. For all the time they spent together and the miles they logged across continents, Dad couldn't even recall The Coyote's real name. I imagined that when the mind becomes so focused on survival, one could lose sight of the smaller details.

"What about these other stamps?" I asked. Placed on top of some of the embassy stamps were smaller markings in a variety of colours and shapes.

"When we left Istanbul, we switched from bus to train. We didn't have to go to an embassy to enter each country anymore. In Europe, agents came on the train and stamped our passports at checkpoints. We did that through Bulgaria, Yugoslavia, and Italy."

"Once you made it to Italy, how soon did you find work?"

"When we got off the train in Venice, we were told by our guide that we couldn't stay there. He didn't say why, and we didn't fight him on it either. He took us to Naples and said, from there, we would go to Malta and maybe find work on a farm. We didn't know it was just a little island. We didn't know any better. We took his word for it. We had to trust him."

Dad paused as if to read my expression. I didn't understand how he could put so much faith in someone he barely knew, how he could place his freedom in another person's hands and surrender all control.

"In order to get things done, you have to trust other people," Dad said. "That applies to family, business...any other part of life. Nothing can ever move forward without trust."

Dad ran his thumb over the gold embossed on the four lions of India's state emblem on the cover of the passport; the gleam of its shine had nearly faded entirely. He opened the passport up to the first few pages again. His large glassy eyes from his passport photo stared back at us. The undone top button of a white dress shirt with intersecting horizontal and vertical lines revealed a thin neck that held up his crown-adorned head. The slight fuzz of a budding beard outlined his jaw. When Dad first got his passport made, the official from the regional office in Chandigarh had written down a few of Dad's identifiers under the photo. Height: 165 centimetres. Eyes: black. Father: Dhanna Singh. That was all he had to his name at the time.

It was in Malta where Dad began to notice fractures in The Coyote's confidence like cracks spider-webbing through glass. The Coyote had always seemed so sure of himself but he didn't know Malta the way he knew Greece or Italy. With funds running low, The Coyote booked a single motel room for himself and all thirteen other men to share in the city of Valletta.

"We didn't think we would be there for more than a few days—just long enough for us to find work on a farm somewhere," Dad said. "We ended up staying there for over two weeks. We were almost out of money so we ate eggs and bread every day, any food that was cheap and could feed a lot of people. The Indian government only let you leave the country with the equivalent of seven American dollars back then. That's the only money I had with me when I left Punjab."

Dad spoke while looking back at the younger version of himself suspended in time in the passport picture. It felt like the man he was now—the person he was in the paat room—was offering counsel to the boy he was in the passport.

"We didn't know where the work was, so we depended on our guide to find jobs for us," Dad explained. "Every day, it was the same thing. He would leave for a few hours, and when he came back, he'd tell us that no one was hiring. Guys in the motel were arguing more, getting into fights. There was a lot of tension. We had to do something."

Dad conspired with Paramjit, Harjinder, and Kewal to break from the rest of the pack and find work on their own. The four of them travelled to the shipyards in Valletta and asked people walking along the docks if any of their ships needed extra workers. One man took the four of them aboard his ship and made tea for them.

"It wasn't until we all finished drinking that he realized we didn't work for him," Dad said. His voice bloomed into laughter. "The man had mistaken us for the only other brown-skinned people working on his ship. When we told him we weren't his employees and that we were looking for work, he sent us to a ship with a big Saudi flag and told us they were hiring. He thought that because we were walking around the shipyard, we were already employed and working in the field. He didn't know that none of us had any work experience." Dad removed his glasses, pinched a corner of the shawl and rubbed it against his lenses. "We didn't tell him either."

***

"Where are you guys from? Punjab?"

Rahim, the captain of the Saudi-owned ship, smoothed out his mustache as he spoke. With his back to the Mediterranean Sea, he leaned against the steel railing that lined the perimeter of his ship.

"Yeah. How did you know?" Satnam asked with a smile. He was twenty-one years old. Hearing someone in Europe talk about Punjab made Satnam feel like home was still real, that it hadn't vanished behind him in the months he'd been away. He turned to Paramjit, Kewal, and Harjinder. They smiled back. "We're all from Jalandhar. What about you?"

"I'm from Jalandhar too," Rahim said. "Born there but raised in Pakistan."

Rahim had been in Europe for the past several years with his wife and children. He had worked aboard various cargo ships and rose in rank to become captain of his own freighter.

"Nice to see someone from back home out here," Harjinder said. He extended a hand to shake Rahim's.

Rahim turned his back to the four of them and looked out at the sea. He lowered his head and sighed. "You fools. Why did you abandon your homes?"

Satnam opened his mouth to respond but didn't know what to say.

"You're out here in this country that doesn't want you and won't accept you," Rahim explained. "You left your parents back home to worry about you while you're out here doing God-knows-what. Do you know what it's like? To be out there in the middle of the ocean?"

The ship bobbed up and down with the rhythm of the waves. Satnam looked out at the waters. The sun kissed the crest of each wave golden. Rahim turned back around to face the four men.

"Come this way," Rahim said, instructing them to follow him.

While giving Satnam, Harjinder, Paramjit, and Kewal a tour of the ship, Rahim explained that he was hiring because his freighter needed repairs before it could be taken out across the oceans again for deliveries. The vessel had been trapped in the Suez Canal since the beginning of the Yom Kippur War in 1973, and was purchased by a Saudi-owned shipping company after the gunfire had settled down. Close to 140 metres in length, the ship's deck contained five large hatchways that cargo was loaded into. Waterproof tarps were drawn and tightened over the hatchways to prevent water from spilling in and soaking the load that sat in the four-storey cargo hold below the surface of the ship's deck. The bridge, where all steering and navigation took place, was located behind the hatchways and ran across the width of the ship. The crew's quarters were located at the back of the freighter. Each member of the crew had their own room which contained the barebones essentials of a bed, a desk, and a cabinet to store sheets, clothes, and any keepsakes they brought along the journey to help remind themselves of home.

"We pay $120 a month—that's American currency," Rahim clarified. He completed the tour and brought them out to the deck again, back in sight of the sea. "We'd need you to start right away. The thing is, we can only afford to hire two of you. I'll give you a few minutes to figure things out. Come by my office when you've made a decision."

Rahim backed away to let them deliberate. The group was silent. Satnam spoke first.

"You should take one of the jobs," he said to Harjinder.

"Me? Why me?" Harjinder replied.

"You're the eldest and the only one of us that's married. You need this job for your family more than we do."

"I think they should take the jobs," Harjinder said, pointing towards Paramjit and Kewal. "You two are family. You shouldn't be separated."

"No, we can't do that," Paramjit pleaded. "Kewal and I don't know how to speak English. We only made it this far because Satnam spoke for us the whole way. We won't survive a day on this ship without you two."

Harjinder nodded. "I understand, but—"

"Wait a minute," Satnam interrupted. His eyes were wide with an idea. "He said $120 a month for two workers, right? What if there was a way for all four of us to work together without any extra cost to Rahim?"

"How would we do that?" Harjinder asked.

"What if we each take half the pay?" Satnam suggested. "$60 a month for each man. That way we can all stay together."

The four of them paused to consider the proposal.

"I think we should ask Rahim and see if he'll go for it," Paramjit said.

"I agree," Kewal added. "Whatever keeps us together."

"I know it's not a lot of money," Satnam noted, "but if we don't want to leave each other, what are our options?"

"It's either this or we all go back to the motel with the rest of the guys," replied Harjinder. "And I'm not going back there."

Satnam led the quartet to Rahim's office and explained his idea. Rahim asked them for a moment alone so he could review some numbers.

Rahim emerged from his office a few minutes later. "This is what you really want to do?" he asked. The four of them nodded in response. "Okay. I did the math and I can afford to give you each $80 a month. Welcome to the team."

***

Satnam, Paramjit, Kewal, and Harjinder never saw The Coyote again. Through the sleepless nights spent aboard packed buses and trains, a fortune paid up front on the strength of nothing but a promise, and a plan that was falling apart the further away they got from home, they felt they didn't owe The Coyote a goodbye.

Satnam didn't ever find out what happened to the other nine men he left behind in Valletta. Though he did take a large pay cut so he and his friends could secure opportunities for themselves, he wrestled with the thoughts of whether he acted selfishly. Satnam was trained from a young age to put the needs of others—his parents, his grandparents, his siblings—before his own. Could he have done more to help the other men in the motel? He didn't know. He didn't have time to think about it either; work started tomorrow morning.

NEW YORK STATE OF MIND

10

CHAPTER TEN

In the summer of 1993, we took a family trip to New York City. Mom, Dad, Vijay, Sardara Chacha Ji, Sukhi Chachi Ji, their baby daughter Simrat, and I piled into a rented Nissan Quest van to travel to Queens, New York to visit an uncle of mine.

In the summers, my parents usually took us to local attractions around Toronto like the CNE, Ontario Place, and Wonderland. This was the first time that we were all leaving our regular haunts to take a vacation. I remember enjoying the ride there, stretching my legs out and laying down in the back seat of the van with a can of Coke in the cup holder next to me. More than seeing any one person, I was looking forward to seeing the city. Having seen the Rangers, Knicks, and Yankees play on TV, I was excited to visit the big landmarks like Times Square, Madison Square Garden, and the Statue of Liberty.

I didn't know the name of the uncle we were going to visit or what our relation was to him. Whether we were actually related to this uncle or he was just a close family friend, I wasn't sure; my family didn't make much of a distinction in how they embraced blood relatives compared to people they knew from the village. Sometimes Mom and Dad would run into long lost relatives at the gurudwara, grocery store, doctor's office, or flea market. They would put everything they were doing on hold to catch up on old times with an uncle or auntie they had lost touch with through migration.

My uncle's apartment in Queens was small. It had two bedrooms and a living room with a brown vinyl couch. The walls were painted topaz blue and the glare from the lightbulbs reflected brightly off the paint. The bathroom had roaches in it and I heard them tap dance across the cold white tiles whenever I pulled the drawstring to turn the light on. Rust outlined the drain of the bathtub that was enveloped by a translucent shower curtain.

Upon arriving in New York, my uncle showed me pictures of his children—a daughter who was my age and a son who was Vijay's age. My uncle said his kids were in Punjab now with their mother, but that he was going to bring all of them to the States to join him one day. I didn't understand why they weren't together. My parents lived with me, Chacha Ji and Chachi Ji lived with Simrat—why couldn't my uncle live with his children?

During our stay, my uncle bunked in one bedroom with his two roommates. My parents, Vijay, and I took the other bedroom, while Chacha Ji, Chachi Ji, and Simrat slept on the fold-out couch in the living room. That first night we arrived in Queens, I was tired from the long drive and tried sleeping, but was kept awake by the adults talking and laughing loudly in the living room. They sounded happy to see each other again. They tried to trace back when they last saw each other, but no one could remember with any certainty. We went to see the Statue of Liberty a few days later but didn't go inside it. We took a picture next to a green, plastic, human-sized replica of the statue and bought a miniature copper figurine to take home with us.

A few years after our trip to Queens, my uncle moved from the US to Rexdale with his wife and children. When I was well into my twenties, I learned more about my uncle, how he got to New York, and why it was so significant for us to go see him. I still didn't know all the details, but I found out more than I knew back in 1993. My uncle's parents had died in a house fire in Punjab when he was just a teenager. As the eldest sibling, he had to take on the role of provider for his brothers and sisters. The family struggled to make ends meet and he left Punjab for Europe to find work, much like Dad did. Through means that weren't explained to me, my uncle was smuggled across the Atlantic Ocean and wound up somewhere in Venezuela. He travelled on foot through Central America and Mexico where he paid someone to take him across the border into the US. Travelling undocumented, he moved along the east coast and eventually made it to Queens where he was allowed to stay under refugee status.

When summer ended and second grade began in September 1993, I told my friends about how I saw the Statute of Liberty, and I brought the copper figurine to class for show and tell. Other kids shared that they went to Wonderland, Blue Jays games, and saw fireworks on Canada Day. I felt like my summer vacation was a bore compared to the things my friends did. Part of me wished I had stayed home and hung out with them instead of going to New York. If I knew then what I know about my uncle now though, I don't think any of my classmates had a summer as eventful or educational as I did.

***

For the first six months of Satnam's employment, Rahim's freighter never left the shipyard. The vessel remained docked in Valletta for the remainder of 1975 and the early months of '76. The crew spent their working hours undoing the damage that the years of rust and war had left behind on the ship. Satnam helped scrub all surfaces and crevices aboard the freighter, and he removed the rice shipment that had spoiled in the bowels of the cargo hold since the fighting ceased several years prior. Picking up some of the basics of ship life from his colleagues, Satnam learned how to operate the cranes that controlled the two anchors at the front of the vessel, and he became an expert in handling the thick mooring ropes aboard the freighter, learning to tie several different types of intricate sailor's knots.

Satnam mainly spent his time painting the exterior of the ship. He would climb down a rope ladder that hung over the edge of the deck while holding a brush in one hand and a can of paint in the other. Little by little, he added a fresh coat to the entire length of the ship. He didn't have a harness to secure himself to the ladder, so windy days left him twisting and swinging in the breeze, fighting to hold on to all of his supplies while trying not to fall into the sea below. Despite these challenges, Satnam didn't mind the work. His mentality was that he would do any job he was asked to do. After the weeks spent travelling through the Middle East and Europe with The Coyote, Satnam was grateful just to have a safe place to stay, as were Harjinder, Paramjit, and Kewal. The money wasn't great but living on the ship saved them the expenses of rent and food. They were getting paid on time, and after taking out some cash to have spending money on hand, they sent the bulk of their earnings back to their families in Punjab.

Word came from Rahim that the repairs were proceeding according to schedule and that the ship would soon be up to code. He informed the crew to prepare for a test run out on the Mediterranean Sea. Sailing during high tide, the waves were choppy that afternoon. The rocky up-down motion made Satnam nauseous. Cold sweat beaded on his forehead. The colour drained from his face. Clenching his stomach with both hands, Satnam staggered on noodled knees to his quarters, collapsed onto all fours, and threw up into the metal toilet. Every exhale felt like it would bring more vomit up with it. The short ferry ride he had taken over six months ago that brought him from Italy to Malta was the only time he had spent aboard a moving vessel; it wasn't enough preparation to help him gain his sea legs.

In between dry heaves, all Satnam could picture was the disappointed look that would have been on his father's face if he were present to witness this. Grabbing the sink to support his body weight, Satnam pulled himself to his feet and rinsed the acidic taste from his mouth. He had to get back to work. Walking through the corridors of the quarters though, he couldn't shake the uneasy feeling in his stomach. He found himself hunched over the toilet again. He couldn't work in the condition he was in. Satnam went to his room and laid down on his bed. His pillow felt cool against his face. He closed his eyes and tried to soothe his stomach against the uneven waters. The door to the room suddenly swung open.

"What the hell are you doing in here?" It was Rahim. He couldn't find Satnam on the deck and had been searching all over the ship to find him.

How long had it been? Satnam thought. How long was I in here?

"I gave you an opportunity," Rahim continued his tirade. "I took a chance on you guys, and now when there's work to be done, I catch you in here sleeping?"

"I wasn't—"

"Get off that bed!" Rahim grabbed Satnam by the forearm and pulled him to his feet. Satnam stood for a moment but felt his legs give out. He sat back down on the edge of the bed.

"I'm sick," Satnam groaned. He cradled his head in his hands.

"No excuses!" Rahim clutched Satnam's wrists, stood him up again, and marched him out the door. "There's work to be done."

96

***

Rahim wasn't satisfied after the ship's trial run. He told the crew that more work was required before the vessel was ready to carry cargo on long hauls again. Satnam and his friends couldn't deal with the slow pace anymore. The longer they stayed in Malta, the more restless they became. They all agreed that they needed to find new jobs aboard ships that were actively making deliveries in order to build their skillset and credibility within the industry.

Just as Harjinder, Paramjit, Kewal, and Satnam had done when they left The Coyote behind to find work on their own, the four friends split up to find out if any other ships in Valletta were hiring. Satnam came across a handful of South Asians roaming the markets during their off-hours and struck up conversation on where they were from, how long they'd been in Malta, and if they had any leads on employment. Glad to help a stranger who carried all the familiarities of home, a couple of Indian sailors introduced Satnam to their captain, a short-statured Egyptian man named Omar. He had a reputation for being hot-tempered, and flexed his authority by berating and cursing at his crew. Omar offered Satnam a job that paid a monthly salary of $400 USD. Satnam gladly accepted.

Paramjit and Kewal found work together on a Lebanese-owned ship. Harjinder couldn't find work elsewhere and ended up staying with Rahim. As the four friends said their farewells, Satnam felt a sorrow for the time that they would no longer share together. However, despite their distance, he believed that they would all be okay no matter where they each ended up. The waters they travelled upon would ensure they stayed connected; the ripples their ships made would always meet and intersect, each wave pushed forward by the same hopes, fears, and dreams they all shared.

***

Working aboard Omar's ship in the spring of 1976, Satnam became fast friends with Raj Kumar. Raj worked down in the engine room and was the same age as Satnam. Raj was a Hindu and belonged to the Dalit caste—the untouchables, deemed to be the lowest rung of the social order in India's prejudicial caste system—and grew up poor. He was born and raised in the village of Bilga in Punjab, about forty kilometres away from Nawan Pind. Raj lived with his mother and step-mother, and took it upon himself to find a way to provide for them ever since his father died. He migrated to Malta about a year before Satnam first left home for Afghanistan, and used similar means of transport to make it to Europe. Raj did various labour jobs in Malta before he found work in the shipping industry.

Omar's ship delivered items such as concrete and iron ore within the vicinity of the Mediterranean Sea to countries like Spain, Portugal, Egypt, and Romania. Raj always made it a point to explore every new city the ship travelled to and took Satnam along with him. Confined to the loud and hot conditions of the engine room for eight hours a day, Raj needed to come up for air to keep himself connected to the world outside of his workstation. He and Satnam picked up bits and pieces of the languages in all the places they visited, becoming just competent enough where they could walk into a market and get food, catch a cab, or find a bar.

Part way through a delivery, Raj came running up from the engine room in a panic. He alerted Omar that one of the boilers had malfunctioned and was no longer producing steam. The ship lost momentum and came to a halt just outside the Gulf of Sirte off the coast of Libya. The ship was rescued by a tugboat after a few hours and towed to Greece for repairs. As the ship pulled into the ports in Piraeus, the city radiated with vibrancy. Multicoloured shipping containers stretched out in countless rows. Orange and blue container cranes stood mightily as if keeping watch over the city. Behind the port were office buildings that extended upward and choked the city skyline. Clusters of quaint white houses saturated the green rolling hills further into the mainland. Eight months after Satnam left home with the intention of going to Greece, he had finally made it to Piraeus.

Since Greece wasn't a planned stop for this ship, all of Omar's crew were issued transit visas. These differed from tourist visas in that they were given to people who were only passing through a country while travelling towards another destination. Under the conditions of the transit visa, Satnam and Raj had to leave Greece within four days. They had nowhere else to go though, and they weren't ready to return to Punjab yet; they hadn't saved up enough money to make this journey to

Europe worthwhile for themselves and their families. Since Omar's ship now needed repairs, Satnam and Raj had four days to either find new jobs or go back home to their villages.

One of the first things Satnam and Raj noticed about Piraeus was the sheer number of Indians they saw walking the streets and working in the shipyards. All the whispers they had heard back in Punjab about Greece being a hotspot for Indians to find work turned out to be true after all. Striking up conversation with a few other Punjabi sailors, Satnam and Raj were directed to a couple of employment agencies that assigned jobseekers to ships in need of crewmembers.

The first agency they visited had a line that stretched outside the building, populated by brown faces all in search of jobs. Satnam and Raj tried another agency a few blocks away and were assigned to work together with a Greek-owned shipping company that had its head office in Piraeus. They were signed to one-year deals that paid $800 USD a month. When Satnam was still back in Nawan Pind, this was the kind of money he was promised he could earn in the West.

Higher pay came with longer hauls. Before their transit visas expired, Satnam and Raj were scheduled for their first assignment aboard a ship that would depart from Cote d'Ivoire to pick up a bulk sugar supply from Rosario, Argentina. They would then return to Europe to deliver the cargo in Lisbon, Portugal.

Satnam and Raj received visas from the French embassy in Greece on August 30, 1976 to fly to Abidjan, Cote d'Ivoire. At the airport in Abidjan, they were greeted by one of their new crewmates who took them to the shipyard to meet their captain, a Greek man named John. In his fifties, clean-shaven, and balding, John's palms were thick, rough, and calloused from years of handling mooring ropes and working at sea.

As their ship pulled away from Cote d'Ivoire and the western coast of Africa disappeared from view, Satnam found himself surrounded only by the vastness of the ocean. He knew that when he was on the Mediterranean Sea with Rahim or Omar, it wouldn't be too long before they'd arrive at their destination and set foot on solid ground again. Sailing across the Atlantic Ocean though, it would take weeks before they saw land. He wondered that if the vessel he relied on for safety was swallowed up by the waves in the middle of the ocean, would anyone even notice? He would soon have his questions answered.

CHAPTER 11

About a month after Mom had returned home from her surgery, I heard a bang on my bedroom door just before 6:00 a.m. followed by a call for help.

"Amrit, wake up!"

It was Dad. More knocks. It sounded like the bottoms of his fists clubbing against the door.

My wife Nuvi and I got out of bed and ran over to Mom's room. We found her collapsed on the floor with her eyes barely open. Dad was in the room with her and dialed 911.

The paramedics soon arrived, their red and white emergency lights slicing through the dark morning. Two paramedics, a man and a woman, clad in fluorescent yellow jackets and dark pants came to tend to Mom. Their heavy black boots squeaked from the morning dew they treaded up the stairs to Mom's room. Picture frames trembled against the walls as they walked through the house.

Dad explained to the paramedics that he had helped bathe Mom earlier that morning, and then went downstairs to get dressed for work. Mom was conscious now, sitting on the carpet and leaning against her bed. Mom added that when Dad was getting ready for work, she went to the kitchen to make herself tea and sweep the floor. When she returned to her room, she felt dizzy and fell over. From downstairs, Dad had heard the thud of her body landing. When he found her, she was unresponsive.

As the paramedics continued to question Mom, Dad gathered all of her medications in a plastic bag and went downstairs again. The look in his eyes was focused and razor sharp. Mom said she was dizzy and weak, but that she felt okay otherwise.

"Why does she sound like that?" the male paramedic said to his colleague.

Since returning home from surgery, Mom had regained her ability to speak, however she couldn't fully open her mouth and she slurred her words. The hole from her tracheostomy still hadn't healed and it was covered with a bandage; when Mom spoke, her speech was backed by the sound of her breath pressing against her dressing like air escaping a bike tire. I explained Mom's condition to the paramedics, stating that she had recently undergone surgery to remove a tumour, and that a few weeks after the operation, doctors had started her on a schedule of radiation and chemotherapy. The treatment immediately took a toll on Mom's body and mind. The morning after she had her first chemo session, she couldn't get out of bed. Unable to muster the strength to walk to the bathroom every time she needed to vomit, Dad had placed a bucket by Mom's bedside; I moistened a towel with cool water and dabbed her forehead until she fell asleep.

Since beginning treatment, Mom was also becoming more forgetful. Her face had gone red with embarrassment one evening when Vijay, Nuvi, and I surprised Dad with a birthday cake. Mom apologized to Dad repeatedly, saying she felt ashamed for spending the entire day with him at Sunnybrook and not remembering what day it was. There were a few nights when Mom forgot to turn off the gas stove before going to bed, leaving it running until Dad or I discovered it early the next morning. I imagined that when the mind becomes so focused on survival, one could lose sight of the smaller details.

The female paramedic placed a gloved hand on Mom's left shoulder to get a better look at the radiation burns on her neck; a bleached out splash of peeling flesh contrasted against the rest of her even skintone.

Dad came back upstairs with a grocery bag full of his and Mom's clothes; he was prepared for another overnight stay at the hospital if necessary. The paramedics checked Mom's heart. Her vitals were normal. They decided not to take her to the hospital for further testing, but advised her to get some rest. They said she was exerting herself to a level that was past the point her body was ready to undertake. Mom said she couldn't rest because she was still in too much pain; she had only made tea and swept the floor as a way to help pass the time. She reasoned that she was only doing the things she normally did at home before she got sick, but the paramedics said she physically wasn't ready for that level of activity yet. Mom, Dad, Nuvi, and I were still learning how to understand this new reality that cancer had thrown upon us. It made us vigilant of every breath or heartbeat of Mom's that sounded slightly out of rhythm.

Without speaking, Dad unpacked Mom's medications from the grocery bag and set them back down on the dresser by her bed.

***

As a teenager, I hated weekends. While most of my friends spent their Fridays making plans to spend the next two days of freedom shooting hoops, playing video games, and watching movies, I often didn't participate. Rather, I couldn't participate—I knew I would be helping Dad with some new project around the house. I didn't know what that project would be yet—planting a garden, re-shingling the roof, renovating the bathroom—I just knew he would need my help to do it. I had to be on standby, keeping my schedule clear and staying at the ready for whenever he required my assistance.

Though I didn't know what we'd be doing come Saturday morning, I already knew how my day would likely start: Mom would run into my room in a panic at 8:30 a.m.—sleeping until nine was considered lazy in my house—to tell me that I needed to hurry outside right now. She'd urge me down the steps in my slumbered state as if the end of the world was looming overhead and we had only seconds to get to the bomb shelter. "Your dad's been working all morning while you've been sleeping," she'd say, laying the guilt trip on thick. Mom would direct me outside and I'd be greeted by the sight of my father elbows-deep in mud, cement, fertilizer, or some other substance that made a sleep-deprived teen wish he was back in calculus class instead. Dad would welcome me with his usual refrain: "Amrit, I need your help." I still hadn't yet wiped the crust out of my eyes, but I already couldn't wait for the day to end.

Dad would sometimes poke fun at me, saying that when his father asked him to do anything on the farm growing up, he had to come running and complete the job as quickly as possible; there was no opportunity for him to sleep in. After working together for a few hours, Dad and I would eventually break for lunch and I'd take the time to slip away and finally hit the showers. Dad would usually remark that we needed to get back to work and I'd just be getting dirty again, so there was no point in taking a shower until after we had finished the job. This was usually the breaking point when I'd be unable to contain my angst any longer. I was already denied my right to sleep in on a Saturday, and had worked for hours in my pajamas without being given the opportunity to change my clothes, brush my teeth, bathe, or eat my cereal. Oh, the injustice. By sundown, we'd either be wrapping up the project, or putting it on pause to repeat the entire process all over again the next morning.

As much as I resisted working with my father at the time, in hindsight, it taught me a lot about the nature of hard work: it often isn't glamorous, and it usually isn't noticed by the others who benefit from it. This was the labour he had taken on his entire life.

The time Dad and I spent working together on the weekends continued into my adulthood and it remained the way we interacted with each other the most. A few years before Mom got cancer, it was when Dad and I were packing away patio furniture for the winter that I told him I wanted to introduce him and Mom to Nuvi, and that we were serious about getting married. It was also when Dad and I were working—cutting vegetables and preparing food as part of the langar to be served at a family kirtan—that I learned he had a baby brother named Satpal who died of a fever before reaching the age of two. Dad said he must have been three or four years old at the time when it happened. When I asked Dad why he didn't ever mention that story to me before, he said it was because we never sat down with each other to have the opportunity to talk about these types of things.

As quiet and inscrutable as I pegged Dad to be, in those instances, I got the sense that there was a part of him that wanted to share the stories of his life; he just needed it occur in the time and spaces where he felt most comfortable. If Dad wasn't in the paat room, being on the job was where it seemed to me that he felt most like himself.

Dad was raised in an era and a culture that saw male vulnerability as weakness. The uncles in my life didn't really talk about their emotions with each other, with their partners, and certainly not with their kids. I felt that the most fruitful conversations I had with Dad took place while working because that was all he was conditioned to do as a man—to get the job done and to provide, quietly and dutifully, without excuses. Having the buffer of work between us allowed me and Dad to talk about things that were personal without having to look each other in the eyes while doing so. We could occupy our hands with our work instead of fully exposing ourselves to a vulnerability that neither of us felt comfortable with and didn't know how to navigate. I learned that just sitting down at a table across from my father wasn't the best way for him to open up and retell his story—we had to physically and actively be doing something.

Mom's radiation schedule required her to be at Sunnybrook every weekday for a total of seven consecutive weeks. Her treatment was set to conclude just before Christmas 2017. With some semblance of routine in Mom's life, Dad returned to his routine too, not only going back to work full-time, but also creating new jobs for himself around the house. I felt the home projects were unnecessary—all the banging and drilling would just disturb Mom—but Dad needed something to do to get his mind on things other than her recovery.

Dad and I cleared out the supplies in the cold storage room in the basement: Coke cans in red cardboard boxes, cases of water bottles, rolls of paper towels, stacks of sectioned recyclable plates with bags of disposable cutlery. His project this weekend was replacing the wobbly free-standing plastic shelves in the storage room with a handmade wooden shelving unit that he would drill directly into the grey cement walls.

"Dad, what are these?" I asked.

In the corner of the storage room, hidden behind some old junk, were two vinyl records still wrapped in their original plastic. We didn't own a record player. What made these records stand out even more though was the artwork. The cover of each record featured Sikh men with dastaars and long beards, and the credits written in Gurmukhi script indicated that these were recordings of kirtan. I had friends who were DJs and vinyl collectors, but none of them had records like these in their catalogues that were connected to our culture and our roots.

"Oh, those," Dad said. He didn't seem as impressed by the records as I was. "I haven't seen those in a while. When I first came to Canada in the eighties and lived with your Massi and Massar, their basement was full of big stacks of those records."

The back covers of the records showed that they were manufactured and distributed by Dhillon & Mahal Bros. in Mississauga, Dhillon being Massar Ji's surname.

"They made these records?" I asked.

"Back when your Massar and his brothers came to Canada in the early seventies," Dad shared, "they wanted to do something special for the Sikh community in Toronto. There weren't a lot of us here back then, but our numbers were growing. My uncles flew in the best musicians and singers from Punjab and booked studio time here locally to record them. They pressed the records themselves and sold them in the area."

"That's so cool," I marvelled. "Why don't they do this type of work anymore?"

"They did well for a few years, but after a while, the records weren't selling. All the stacks they had in the basement was the inventory that was left over."

I likened these records to Dad's old passports, considering them to be valuable family heirlooms that told so much about our history. However, for reasons only known by Dad's generation, the records were kept hidden and unspoken of for decades. I set the records aside and swept out the cobwebs from the corners of the storage room. Dad held his measuring tape in hand and had a pencil tucked between his ear and his orange parnaa.

"I guess they were trying something new," Dad added. "Sometimes it works, sometimes it doesn't. Like when I got to Greece."

"What was Greece like?" I asked.

"When I got my first job on a ship there, I worked a lot in the kitchen. That was the first time I had ever cooked for anyone," Dad laughed. While he was growing up, Dhadhi Ji did all the cooking for everyone who lived with the family in Nawan Pind. "I learned how to make eggs and pasta and Greek-style potatoes. I learned how to make spaghetti. I was the one who taught your mom how to make spaghetti when we came to Canada years later. Raj was working down in the engine room again."

Dad used his foot to secure one end of the measuring tape where the wall met the floor, and I guided the other end of the tape to the ceiling. He used the pencil to tag a series of lines on the wall.

"I remember the first time I steered the ship," Dad said. He squinted as he studied the lines he had just drawn. The lead from the pencil didn't stand out much against the grey paint on the walls. "This was when we were still on the way to Argentina from the Ivory Coast."

"Did you have to do some sort of training for that?" I placed a level against the wall between two of the lines that Dad drew. The green bubble bounced and wobbled before settling to signify that things were even.

"They asked me one day if I knew how to steer, so I steered," Dad explained. "I was supposed to get some training, but I never did."

"That's so dangerous. Why would you say yes if you didn't know how to do it?"

"I came there to work, so I told myself I would do any job that they asked me to do. I didn't feel like I was in a position to say no to them; I needed the job and the money. If I didn't know how to do something, I would learn."

Dad picked up a drill and drove it into the concrete where a few pencil markings intersected. He leaned into it with all of his body weight, one hand on the drill handle, and the other pushing the back of the drill into the wall until the steel tip broke through the resistance of the concrete. Dust floated and settled in the sweat on his face.

"I was having dinner with Raj one evening and the captain asked if one of us could fill in for a shift at the wheel," Dad explained. "Shifts at the helm were only two hours. That wasn't too long, so I said I'd do it. He wanted me on the 4:00 a.m. shift so I felt like I had plenty of time to learn from the person who would be steering before me."

Dad handed me the drill and asked me to make the next hole.

"Before I went to bed that night," he continued, "I talked to the guy who would be steering on the shift just before me. I asked him to wake me up at 2:00 a.m. when his shift started so that I could watch and learn from him to get a better feel for things before it was my turn to do it on my own. The other driver didn't wake me up though. I overslept. I jumped out of bed and ran to the helm just a few minutes before my shift was supposed to begin."

I drilled a hole into the wall, and another equidistant from the last.

"He started showing me all the controls," Dad described, "but it was too much information for me to make sense of in such a short time. I was with him for maybe five minutes and then my shift started. It was my turn to steer by myself."

"You didn't crash the ship, did you?" I remarked.

Dad's laughter echoed off the walls. We lifted a piece of wooden shelving that we had assembled earlier in the day that ran the length of the storage room. I held it against the wall and Dad drilled in the screws to anchor the wood in place. Yellow and white wood shavings curled and fell to the floor.

"Thankfully, the water was very calm that morning," Dad said. "I couldn't get the ship to go straight though. I tried to follow the compass, but I kept going either ten degrees too far in one direction or the other. The officer there with me kept asking me if everything was okay. He was so confused why I couldn't steer properly."

Dad and I lifted another bed of wood and drilled it to the wall to create a second layer of shelving a few feet above the first. Dad grabbed the shelf with both hands and pulled down. It didn't shake.

"Look," Dad said. He smiled at his handiwork. "How strong. You could put any weight on that and it won't break."

He took a lot of pride in his work. It meant a great deal to him to prepare and execute things with patience and care so they would be built to last. Even when things occurred that he couldn't prepare for, when the situation required a base and instinctual response—like when Mom had collapsed—he still operated with a mindset focused on action. I would soon discover that this way of thinking was developed during Dad's time at sea. It was honed when he was given the choice between living and perishing, and he somehow found a way to carry himself and the people around him to survival.

CHAPTER
Tame the Storm
TWELVE

At the start of second grade, my parents signed me and Vijay up for swimming lessons in the evenings. Dad wasn't ever back home from work early enough to go to the classes with us, so Mom would take us through the catwalk lined with fallen yellow leaves towards the pool at Westwood Secondary School just before dark. In its descent, the sun painted orange and purple streaks across the sky.

Inside, the turquoise water of the pool was surrounded by rectangular, off-white tiles. A metal ladder leading up to a blue plastic slide stood over the deep end, and a shelf lined with multi-coloured life jackets, flutter boards, and pool noodles was positioned along the wall by the shallow end. By the time the classes started, the sun had fully gone down and only darkness came in through the square windows that ran parallel to the length of the pool. I didn't really enjoy coming to my lessons. I liked playing in the water with my friends, but I didn't ever get the hang of swimming. I hated the way the smell of chlorine stayed in my hair and how my fingers stayed pruned for hours after each class.

"Alright guys, grab your floating boards and get in the water," my instructor said at the start of one of the lessons. He always sounded more excited than us to be there.

The instructor made us all line up at one side of the shallow end. "On your backs, people! Remember to keep kicking, and I'll see you at the other end," he hollered with a wink and a smile. The shrill yelp of his whistle punctured the air. I tucked my red flutter board under my chin, hugged it to my chest and leaned backwards. Water was in my ears.

"You're doing great! Keep going!" my instructor shouted. I wasn't sure if he was talking to me in particular, or just offering general encouragement to the class. My legs pulsated up and down just as he taught us to do, but I didn't ever feel like I was doing it right.

"Okay, now let go of your flotation devices," he directed.

I held on to my board and continued kicking and counting the support beams in the ceiling.

"Let go!" he shouted again.

He couldn't have been talking to me, I thought. Out of the corner of my eye, I saw his hairy legs leading up to his red shorts. He walked along the width of the shallow end at the same speed that I swam.

"You're doing fine, just let go," he said.

"I'm not ready yet," I called back over the splashes and shouts of the other students. My fingers squeezed tighter around the board.

"It's okay," he tried to reassure me. "Don't be scared. It's just a little bit of water. Relax your body. Humans can float."

With my legs kicking, I uncrossed my arms and released the board. My legs felt heavy and sunk like they had cinder blocks tied to them. I tried to keep my eyes on the support beams in the ceiling but my head was soon pulled under. Searching for safety, I planted my feet on the floor of the pool and forced my head through to the surface.

Coughing and spitting water out of my mouth, I rubbed my wrinkly fingers against my burning eyes. "You said humans can float!" I shouted.

I waddled towards the edge of the pool and pulled myself out. I only made it through another lesson or two before I told my parents that I wanted to quit the program. Water scared me. As much as I tried, I couldn't bring myself to surrender to it. I didn't want to drown.

***

The TV in the ship's dining quarters only got reception when the freighter was close to land. As dockworkers in Rosario, Argentina loaded the cargo hold with thousands of tons of sugar destined for Lisbon, Portugal, Satnam sat next to Raj and Captain John in the dining hall. They all stared in unison at the Zenith propped in the corner of the room to catch up on the news. The newscaster spoke in Spanish, but the crew still got the message: a storm was looming over the Atlantic.

"Are you worried?" Raj asked John.

"Yes and no," John said after an audible sigh. "I've been through storms before. You don't ever feel good about it, even when you know it's coming. We just have to be prepared." Static interrupted the television feed before the picture returned to focus.

Despite the news reports, the first half of the two-week journey from Argentina to Portugal had gone off without a hitch outside of some rough waters. However, John received several communications that informed him of recent tragedies that involved other ships that had travelled along this same path. On some vessels, waves had swept crewmembers off their feet and pulled them into the ocean; other freighters were capsized with all crew aboard perishing.

After making a brief stop in Cape Verde to refuel, the speed of the winds intensified along the home stretch towards Portugal. Angry storm clouds punished the ship with a deluge of cold rain. The waves had become increasingly more turbulent. Nobody could sleep; those who tried to rest were thrown from their beds by the overpowering force of the waters. The ocean was hypnotizing to watch. Satnam often observed in awe as waves surged upwards with all of the pressure and darkness of their depths and cut through the skies. Some of the waves only appeared threatening, elevating to the brink of a dizzying peak before being swallowed back down. Other waves manifested and crashed violently. The waters swelled and ascended in slow motion. The days seemed to last longer. Everything moved slower at sea.

John kept the ship running as orderly as possible through the storm, and had his crew stick to their regular shifts and rotations. The unspoken assumption among management and crew alike though was that anyone could be called upon at a moment's notice to offer additional support.

John entered the dining hall. He pulled back the hood from his yellow raincoat and wiped the water from his face. "Satnam, I need your help."

"Yes, sir?" Satnam rose from his seat.

"I need you to take over at the helm for a few hours. Can you do it?"

The embarrassment from Satnam's first shift at the wheel still weighed on his mind, but there wasn't time to think about that now. John needed all hands available if they were to make it to the other side of the storm alive. Satnam followed his captain outside across the ship's deck towards the bridge. They held hands for stability against the winds that howled at them. Knees bent and backs hunched, they stayed low the ground. They took short, quick steps to brace themselves against the elements. Raging waves roared from behind the steel railing of the deck's perimeter like lions behind cage bars.

There wasn't much space inside the helm to maneuver. The white ceiling was just a few feet above Satnam's head. Windows lined the three sea-facing walls. Black rubber squares were embedded in the white tiles of the floor to offer him traction. The steering wheel was stationed at the front of the room next to a circular compass used to navigate the ship.

Satnam stood behind the wheel and peered out into the stormy conditions. All he saw was an endless landscape of grey that devoured all light, unable to separate where the waters ended and the overcast clouds began. Before he could gather his bearings, a wave elevated the back end of the ship and submerged the bow under water. The gravity sent Satnam's ribs and sternum crashing into the wheel. The nose of the vessel came back up for air. Satnam steadied himself.

"Do you want to stop?" John asked. "I can get somebody else—"

"No, it's okay," Satnam waved him off. "I can do it."

The ship struggled to make any progress against the resistance of the waters; ten feet forward and twenty feet back, Satnam thought. Waves raised the front of the vessel skyward, giving Satnam a view of the darkened heavens above. John let out a victorious belly laugh when the freighter returned to an upright position.

Their reprieve was short lived as a wave emerged from the ocean directly in front of them. A wall of water climbed over three storeys high. A silence fell over the ship. Satnam braced for the inevitability of contact.

The impact of the crash flung Satnam and John to the other side of the room. Sheets of water poured down the windows of the helm. Satnam got up and waited for the streams to drain away until he could see the bow again. The compass showed coordinates that Satnam didn't recognize. The impact of the collision had forced the vessel off course. Wrestling with the wheel, he turned the ship back towards their destination. The waves looked like mountains. Each jagged crest the ship maneuvered past was followed by another one that reached even higher into the sky. Through the mist, Satnam spotted a beam of light in the distance. Land was within reach.

"We made it!" John shouted, slapping Satnam on the shoulder in encouragement. "Just a little further."

The storm-battered ship pulled into the port in Lisbon. The crew gathered outside the helm and waited for Satnam to emerge. When he came out, each man took turns shaking his hand in gratitude.

"I can't thank you enough," one of them said. "I don't know how you did it," said another. They all wore smiles, grateful to stand on solid ground, thankful they weren't buried with the other vessels claimed by the ocean.

John took Satnam aside, placed a hand on each of his shoulders, and stared him square in the face. "Satnam, I've been doing this a long time. I've never seen a storm like that. For a while, I didn't think I was going to see civilization again. What you did today—"

"Really, it was nothing," Satnam stopped him. "The only way to pass the storm is to go through it. I just did my part."

***

A few months later, Satnam's ship was sailing through the Suez Canal. The pathway was so tight that whoever was steering couldn't see the sides of the canal from where they stood at the helm, so a local harbour pilot was assigned to help the vessel get through the narrow and congested passage. Sailor after sailor failed to get through the canal, each of them bumping the sides of the ship into the walls of the passageway despite the instructions given by the pilot. Six different men took their turn at the wheel and all were unable to maneuver the craft through the canal's slender opening. The pilot grew agitated, unsure of how he could communicate his directions with any more clarity. Eventually, John called upon Satnam to try his hand at the wheel. Satnam succeeded in steering the freighter smoothly through the canal without any thuds or thumps along the way.

Satnam saw his experience in the Suez Canal as a metaphor for the past year of his life at sea: he chased opportunity through the narrowest of openings and somehow, he kept making it to the other side. As accustomed as he had grown to living with strangers from different parts of the world and finding brotherhood amidst the uncertainty of the ocean, home was calling. All of this work Satnam had undertaken was for the benefit of his family, and he would soon have a chance to reunite with the people who raised him. Though he had seen the world, the village awaited his return.

CHAPTER

✛

Politics as Usual

✛

CHAPTER THIRTEEN THIRTEEN

Growing up, my parents didn't ever discuss race with me. In my mind, it felt like their belief was—by virtue of being born in Canada—my citizenship would grant me immunity from discrimination, and I would be seen as someone who belonged in this country. However, as a kid in the nineties who saw news reports of Rodney King and Dudley George on TV at a young age, I learned that there was something darker behind the narrative that North America was a post-racial land of promise. When researching my own historical blindspots and examining the relationship between Sikhs and Canada, I found that no matter how hard we tried to ingratiate ourselves with this country, we were still denied that sense of belonging.

The first 5000 settlers from India arrived in British Columbia between 1904 and 1908, the majority of whom were Sikh men from Punjab. They found work primarily in railway construction and forestry, and faced discrimination immediately as Sikh labourers were paid less than their white colleagues for doing the same work.

Anti-Asian sentiment towards Chinese, Japanese, and Indian people was widespread in Canada. In 1885, the Canadian government instituted a Chinese Head Tax, a fee charged to each Chinese person who migrated to the country. In 1903, this tax was increased to $500 as a way to deter further immigration from China. In Canadian media, Asians were portrayed as carrying disease and being uncivilized, and were deemed incapable of adapting to the Canadian way of life. As India was still under British colonial rule at the time, Indians were considered British subjects and had the right to vote in the elections of other colonies. However, despite their shared commonwealth status, the Canadian government changed the laws so that Indians not born of Anglo-Saxon parents could not vote in Canada, hold public office, serve on juries, or find work in law, accounting, and the pharmaceutical industry. This discrimination fueled the Anti-Asiatic Riots in Vancouver in 1907 where businesses owned by Chinese and Japanese people were damaged, and Asians were assaulted in the streets.

Though Sikhs were spared the worst of the riots, other laws were changed that impacted further migration of people from India into Canada. On January 8, 1908, the Canadian government issued a policy that all new immigrants seeking to enter the country had to travel by a continuous and uninterrupted journey. At the time, it was impossible to travel from India to Canada via direct passage—the distance was just too far to make by ship without stopping in Japan or Hawaii along the way to refuel. This policy, racist more so in its details than in its explicit wording, slowed immigration of Indians to Canada from a rate of 5000 people between 1904 and 1908, to just 118 people between 1908 and 1920. These regulations came at a time when the Canadian government was welcoming large numbers of European immigrants, 400 000 of which entered Canada in 1913 alone. In the same vein as the Chinese Head Tax, immigrants from India needed to have $200 in their possession when entering Canada, while European immigrants only needed $25.

H.H. Stevens, an alderman for the city of Vancouver, stated that "Canada shall remain white, and our doors shall be closed to Hindoos as well as to other Orientals." Soon after that, it wasn't just enough to put up barriers to prevent Sikhs from coming into Canada; the Canadian government sought to expel those who had already migrated. In 1908, a delegation of Canadian ministers and immigration officials were sent with Nagar Singh and Sham Singh, a pair of local Sikhs from British Columbia, to visit what is now modern-day Belize to explore the possibility of resettlement of Sikhs who were residing in Canada. The Canadian government framed the move as being in the best interest of Sikhs, stating that they would be better off in a warmer climate that was similar to Punjab. Nagar Singh and Sham Singh rejected the move on the grounds that resettlement would subject Sikhs to poor living conditions and exploitation for cheap labour by another arm of the British empire.

As the decades rolled on and the original Sikh settlers established themselves in their communities, younger generations inherited their parents' struggles. One notable example was that of Ajit Kaur, the daughter of farm owner Mehar Singh who had migrated from Punjab to Kelowna, British Columbia in 1907. After Mehar died, Ajit decided in 1946 to sell the family farm and purchase a house in the city with her children. However, the sale of the house was blocked by white residents in the community. Ajit's neighbours held the fear that her presence there would result in a flood of more South and East Asian people relocating to the city, which they felt would lower their property value, and deteriorate the security and character of the area.

Almost seventy years later, my hometown of Brampton had its own Ajit Kaur moment. In April 2014, several neighbourhoods in the city were covered in flyers distributed by a group known as Immigration Watch Canada. Titled as "The Changing Face of Canada," the flyers featured a photo of a group of white people looking calm and seated in an orderly manner, juxtaposed with a picture of a group of Sikhs at a protest looking angry. The flyer referenced the decrease in 'mainstream Canadians' in Brampton's population in recent years, and asked 'Is this really what you want?' Another flyer circulated in March 2015 called the decrease in Brampton's European population a 'white genocide.'

Though my wife Nuvi worked from home during September 2017 to help take care of Mom after the surgery, Nuvi was mostly absent during the months that followed. Though she wished she could be home more, no one held it against her—we understood the history she was making. Nuvi worked as a Field Director on the national campaign that helped elect Jagmeet Singh as the leader of the New Democratic Party, the first time a person of colour had ever been elected leader of a federal party in Canada. Bachittar Massar Ji had told me about the importance of taking up space and fighting for your voice to be heard when he took his anti-discrimination case to the labour board back in the seventies; the work Nuvi was doing with Jagmeet was an extension of that. However, some of the struggles Massar Ji had faced back then still played out during Jagmeet's campaign. Nuvi was present when a white woman stormed the stage at one of Jagmeet's town hall meetings and accused him of being an Islamic extremist and terrorist sympathizer. The woman was disruptive, yelled, stuck her finger in Jagmeet's face, and threatened to call the cops if anyone put their hands on her. Nuvi was one of the people who helped remove the woman from the scene.

After the conversation I had with Massar Ji about the discrimination he faced living in Toronto in the seventies, and how Dad told me he had to cut his hair to protect himself before entering Europe, I was curious to know if Dad faced any racism in his travels. He wasn't a politician; he was just a person working out on the expanse of the ocean. If it could happen to someone leading a federal party, I reasoned that it must have happened to Dad at some point too.

"Did you deal with any racism when you worked on the ships?" I asked.

"Not from my coworkers," Dad said without hesitation. "I worked with people from all over the world—Pakistan, Ethiopia, Greece, Somalia, Italy—nobody on the job treated anyone else differently because of their race. We all looked out for each other."

Dad and I were in the kitchen washing teacups—the nice cups we only brought out when we had company over. A few guests had visited us earlier in the day to see Mom. They had heard about her recent fall and wanted to see how she was doing. Having too many people over made Mom tired. I wanted to limit the number of visitors that came to the house so Mom could rest more, but Dad said it was rude in Punjabi culture to tell someone they couldn't come over—if they want to come, let them come, he said. After our guests had left, Mom tried to sleep upstairs.

"I remember one time in Egypt," Dad explained. "Our ship was docked far out from the port in Alexandria. Two of my crewmates wanted to go into the city to explore. They were taking a rowboat to go from our ship to the town. They asked me to go with them so that I could row the boat back to the ship after they left. I didn't know how to row a boat—"

"But you did it anyway?" I cracked a smile at Dad, my head still down towards the dishes.

The sink faced a window that overlooked the ravine behind our house. Evergreen trees still carried remnants of the last snowfall on their limbs. The weak sun pushed muted light through a sky that was drained of colour. An incense stick was placed near the sink in a brass stand. The tower of grey ashes forming on the tip was separated from the rest of the black stick by a glowing orange border.

"I figured I would watch them row on the way to the city," Dad said. "I would learn from them that way, and I thought I would be okay to row back to the ship on my own. That's how I learned everything on the ship—by watching and then actually doing it. I didn't think it would be that hard." Dad applied more soap to his sponge; the thick blue liquid bled out over the green scrubbing exterior. "So I watched them row. It looked easy. The two guys got off in Alexandria and I had to row back by myself. The sun was starting to go down and it was very windy. I tried rowing straight but I couldn't direct the boat towards my ship. The wind kept pushing me farther away."

"How did you make it back then?" I asked.

"I didn't know what else to do so I started yelling for help. Someone from a different ship heard me—a Somalian guy—and he came on his own rowboat to save me. When he reached me and I explained how I got out there, he told me never to do that again. So much could have gone wrong. I'll never forget that." Dad finished soaping the last of his dishes and shook his hands. Pellets of water rapped against the sink. "Another thing that I remember," he continued, "was a delivery to Nigeria."

Shortly after Dad had made it through the storm on the Atlantic Ocean and arrived in Portugal, his ship carried a cargo of cement from Spain to Lagos. Due to an error in the order, the shipment was larger than the port's receiving capacity could handle. Dad's ship stayed docked off the coast of Lagos for two months before he could unload. Outside of cleaning the ship and doing general maintenance, no work could be done until more receiving space in the port opened up. After a few days, Dad and Raj ventured into Lagos to explore.

"I was working and sending money back to Punjab then," Dad detailed. "The dock workers in Lagos had a different job than I did, but they were still in the shipping industry. I thought we were all making similar money. When I went to Nigeria, it hadn't been that long since it was under colonial rule. The British took so many resources before they left. A lot of Nigerian people were struggling then. I saw some dock workers looking through trash cans and dumpsters to find food."

"For survival," I said.

I placed the last cup down and ran my hands under the warm water to remove the excess soap. Dad dried his hands on the towel that hung from the oven door. He paused for a moment. Without a word, Dad went upstairs. I traced the sound of his footsteps up to Mom's room. It sounded like he stopped at her door, but didn't go in, like he was checking to see if she was still breathing and fighting.

***

In the winters, crews had to be careful when navigating through frozen waters the further north they ventured. In January 1977, Satnam's ship was stuck in the ice of the North Sea by East Germany. He was close enough to shore to see the city and all the lights teasing him in the distance, but couldn't do anything to get closer to land. After being immobile for fifteen days and radioing out to the mainland, an ice-breaking tugboat pulled the ship to shore.

While Satnam was at sea, communication with the family in Punjab was done by writing letters. Nobody in Nawan Pind had a phone. Every time the family received a new letter from Satnam, they huddled around the envelope together and admired the colourful designs on the stamps sent from places of the world they couldn't pronounce or locate on a map. The letters were almost prose-like given the heartfelt ways in which Satnam addressed his parents. *"To my beloved and respected mother and father,"* he would begin. In the letters, Satnam offered assurances that he was eating well and enjoying the work, and estimated when he might be coming home. The family would be in tears by the time they finished reading.

Satnam's parents sent him letters through the post office in the village of Nussi, and addressed them to his shipping company's head office in Piraeus. Based on the ship's scheduled route, letters would be mailed by staff in Greece to the port that Satnam's ship was scheduled to arrive at next. Upon entering East Germany, Satnam received a letter from his family announcing that his sister Jasvir's wedding had been set for April 1, 1977. To assure Satnam that the wedding was real, Jasvir's post-script noted that this was not an April Fools' joke.

As was customary in Punjabi culture, Satnam told Raj about the wedding and invited him to attend. He wasn't expecting Raj to actually say yes. Raj said that he considered Satnam to be his brother, and by extension, he felt like his own sister was getting married. Satnam and Raj told Captain John that they would be finishing up work in a few months to go back home.

While he was out in the world, Satnam held on to the things that connected him to the home he knew. When he sailed to Portugal, he watched the movie *Sholay* in theatres. When he sailed to Kuwait, he

120

bought cassettes of Bollywood soundtracks to listen to in his quarters. Now that he was returning to the village after nearly two years away, with Raj at his side, he was bringing a piece of the world back home with him.

***

Satnam stood between two suitcases in the kitchen of his family's home in Nawan Pind. It was March 1977. He was twenty-three years old. Only a few days remained until Jasvir's wedding.

"What are you wearing?" Dhanna grumbled. Satnam was dressed in brown leather platform shoes with a three-inch stacked heel, skin-tight dark blue jeans, and a white Lee's muscle shirt.

"It's the style, Dad," Satnam replied.

Dhanna shook his head. "What happened to your hair? Is that the style too? Your dastaar isn't good enough for Greece? And what's with that Hindu guy? Raj, is it? Why did you bring him here?"

Sampuran waved a hand at Dhanna to get him to keep his voice down. Raj was outside in the verandah introducing himself to Satnam's siblings. Sampuran turned to Satnam and placed a hand on his cheek as if to feel he was really back home. "It's good to see you, son," she said. Tears moistened her eyes.

"It's good to see you too, Mom." They shared an embrace. "The house looks great."

Life carried on in the village while Satnam was gone. Jasvir was now the parental figure to her younger siblings and inherited the role that Satnam had previously occupied. Dhanna provided Jasvir with money to purchase seeds and supplies from the markets. She'd travel on her own and bring all the goods back home in the wicker basket attached to her bicycle. Satnam's brothers Mohinder and Sardara had taken up more responsibility on the farm, putting in long hours in the fields with Dhanna. Sardara had even severed a digit off his finger in an accident with a piece of machinery on the farm much like Satnam had done in his childhood. Kuldip, the baby of the family, was becoming an accomplished athlete and performed well at school in track and long jump.

The money Satnam sent home helped the family in big ways and small. Gone were the house's mud walls that were susceptible to inclement winds and rain—they were replaced by concrete. Dhanna was able to rent out tractors and other farm equipment to tend to his crops, while Kuldip had a brand new red bike to get to and from school. Their household was the first in Nawan Pind to own a TV. The village buzzed with excitement on Thursday nights as friends and strangers alike congregated around the black and white glow of the television to watch Bollywood films.

The family was also able to buy tiny luxuries they couldn't afford before. Sampuran kept a tin full of cookies made with refined sugar locked in a pantry away from the prying hands of her children. She only brought the cookies out when the family entertained guests and served tea.

Satnam pulled one of his suitcases onto the kitchen counter and unzipped it, revealing stacks of bills totalling over 80 000 rupees.

"What is this?" Sampuran asked. She placed both hands on her head.

"I worked for it," Satnam said. "It's for us."

"You can't keep this money here." Sampuran closed the suitcase and looked around the room as if there were spies watching them. "There are going to be so many people coming in and out of the house for the wedding."

"She's right," Dhanna chimed in. "It's not safe."

Satnam tried to offer them assurance. "Trust me, nobody is going to steal this money." He picked up a red shawl from the counter and unfolded it.

"What are you doing with that?" Sampuran protested.

Satnam wrapped the bills in the shawl, knotted the corners of the fabric together, and tossed it out of view atop the same cabinet the cookies were locked in.

"Trust me," Satnam said. "It's safe. Nothing is going to happen to that money." He put his hands on Sampuran's shoulders and led her out of the kitchen towards the verandah. "Come. Let's all spend time together as a family."

***

Jasvir's wedding was held at the family home in Nawan Pind under a tent in the verandah. The walls of the tent were lined with fulkari-printed drapes bordered by golden tinsel. Hundreds of guests attended from all over Punjab. For Satnam, this entire event was a family reunion as much as it was a wedding. He took the time to catch up with relatives and friends that he hadn't seen since he first left home for Europe. He also paid back Gurmukh Mamma Ji for the money he had contributed in helping Satnam afford The Coyote's initial fee.

After the wedding, Jasvir left Nawan Pind to live with her husband and in-laws. Satnam would soon be leaving home as well. Just as he had foretold, nobody found the money on top of the cabinet, but that cash wasn't enough to sustain the family in the long term. He had more work to do and the waters would call his name once again.

UNATTACHED

14

By the end of November 2017, I was still working with the non-profit organization while also completing my internship at the mental health agency. Despite the busy schedue, I still regularly had a few days off during the week. On those days, I drove Mom to Sunnybrook for her radiation appointments.

Radiation took place in the basement of the hospital, which was undergoing renovations. Exposed drywall panels lined both sides of the narrow corridor leading to Mom's radiation room. The state of the hospital basement made it hard to discern whether the building was experiencing reconstruction or demolition; with the toll that the treatment was taking on Mom's body, I wondered the same of her. She had always had a slender build, but since commencing with radiation and chemo, she was losing weight and withering away. Her hospital gown hung from her rail-thin frame like sails on a mast. There were a few occasions at home when her rings had slipped right off her fingers. Her left shoulder—the side where the radiation was being focused—had lost all structure and slumped downward.

Mom was greeted by a nurse and taken into the radiation room. I sat in the only chair at this end of the basement and waited for her to complete her session. After about half an hour, Mom exited the radiation room dragging her left foot behind her. Her eyes were open but her expression was blank.

"Mom..." I tried to get her attention but she walked right past me as if she didn't hear me. She looked disembodied—physically present, but the light inside of her seemed to be turned out.

"Mom." I spoke louder this time, hoping my voice would snap her out of her trance.

She stopped walking. I held her hand and guided her back to the change room. I felt her pulse beating through her fingertips; her light was still on inside somewhere. As much as the doctors had told us that Mom was taking to the treatment well, it felt like the radiation was breaking her down and corroding her. It seemed that even after the cancer had been cut out of her, she still owed it a debt; treatment was stealing pieces of life away from her until her balance was even.

***

Cancer treatment causes the body to experience a desiccation. The radiation dried up Mom's ability to produce saliva; she kept a spray bottle close by to moisten her mouth every few minutes. The skin on the back of her neck was white and flaky, and looked like scorched earth where no hair could sprout. The hydromorphone she was prescribed to deal with the pain of the surgery caused constipation and stomach cramps. To manage the dryness, a nurse came by the house every day for the two months that Mom was on chemo and radiation to hook her up to an IV and help her rehydrate.

Though Dad was back at work, he shifted his hours around so he could take Mom to her appointments at Sunnybrook on the days when I wasn't available. Some days, Dad started work at four or five in the morning and came back home at noon to pick Mom up and take her to the hospital for treatment at 1:00 p.m. He was running himself ragged and put the onus on himself to take on the largest share of the responsibility. Sometimes when I came home from work in the afternoons, I'd find Dad lying on the floor in the paat room trying to recharge and steal a few extra minutes of sleep.

We wouldn't know whether Mom would need more chemo or radiation until she finished this first round at the end of December and met with Dr. Higgins for a check-up in April 2018. We wished we had an answer now but we still had the rest of the winter to get through. Still, Mom had made it this far. She was a fighter.

Since the cancer diagnosis, the thought of death was always in the back of my mind—how close it was, and whether we were doing enough to care for Mom to keep her around for another sunrise. There had been another incident at home where Mom got dizzy and fell over again. We called the paramedics and they took her to the hospital this time, but the doctors didn't find anything wrong with her. "Somehow I keep being saved," Mom said. I couldn't tell if she was grateful or disappointed.

Nobody in the family talked about what might happen if Mom didn't survive this illness—at least, no one talked about it out loud. The collective hope of the family and medical staff was that Mom would come out scarred and weakened but still standing. We just wanted her to get through treatment and be cleared as cancer-free in April; it was hard to plan and think about a future any further than that.

The closeness of death can make one reflect. Did you do, see, and accomplish everything you imagined for yourself in life? Did you regret the way you spent your time? How deeply did you love the people around you? Death brings about a finality that we can't prepare for.

Dad had told me that his Dhadhi died in 1976 when he was out working on the ships. He didn't learn of her passing until he came back home to the village in 1977 for his sister Jasvir's wedding. Dad said it was hard for him not to be there when his grandmother passed, but there was nothing he could do—he had to work. I pondered whether maybe it would be easier not to be around when someone who I loved was dying. I had seen it with my own grandparents as both Dhadhi Ji and Dhadha Ji had long and agonizing descents until they reached their final days. Watching death slowly pillage one's body and mind, as I was witnessing in Mom's illness, was hard to be a spectator for.

When I was a kid and Dad wanted me to start reading Gurbani and getting in touch with the Sikh philosophy and way of life, he got me a book that had English translations of the scripture. In reading through those books, I noticed how Gurbani mentioned death constantly: how we shouldn't forget it, and how we shouldn't live life attached to this illusory and impermanent world. It was different than how death was discussed in Western media and spirituality. Here, death was cruel. Phrases about the good dying young, and allusions to the deceased being in heaven and watching down on us were quoted to help people reason with mortality. In Sikhi though, death was a natural fact of life. Death was an equalizer that royals and beggars alike would fall to. I struggled with reconciling the two perspectives on death. The thought of being unattached felt cold to me, like I shouldn't engage with the world or care for the people around me. I didn't understand what it meant to view death through an unattached lens until my grandparents died.

**

On June 5, 2013, Dad was scheduled to leave on a flight from Toronto to attend a funeral. Dad's mentor, the man responsible for helping him comprehend and apply Sikh scripture in everyday life, had died. No one knew how old he was for sure, but all estimates from the people that knew him the longest pegged him at over a hundred.

I knew Dad's mentor only as Baba Ji, a term of respect used to refer to an elder in one's family and community. I first became aware of Baba Ji in the mid-nineties when he lived in Brampton and we still lived in Malton. Dad would travel to him straight after work and they'd spend hours together meditating and discussing lines of Gurbani at length. When Dad had heard the news of his teacher's passing, he booked the earliest flight he could find to attend the funeral in Punjab where Baba Ji had spent the last several years of his life running a school and orphanage.

Dad and I didn't say much to each other on the drive to the airport. He stared out the window with his head turned away from me. Traffic was heavy along the 427 and the flow of cars slowed to a stop. I turned off the air conditioning and opened the windows halfway. Dad preferred the natural air to the AC. I couldn't think of any words that would console him. We didn't really do that for each other anyway.

When we got to the airport, I pulled the car over beneath the awning and removed Dad's suitcase from the trunk. "Call us when you get there," I said. "Have a safe flight." He extended the handle on his suitcase, rolled it behind him, and disappeared into the airport.

On my drive back home, while still stuck in traffic, my phone buzzed. The caller ID showed that it was Dad on the other line. Keeping one eye on the road, I answered the call. Before I could speak though, Dad's voice cut me off.

"Amrit, I need you to come to the hospital," he said.

"Hospital? Why? What's wrong?" We were just at the airport. He was supposed to leave the country in a few hours. He wasn't making sense.

"It's your Dhadhi. I'll explain when you get there. The hospital in Brampton. Just come now. Quickly."

"What about your flight?"

"I'm not going. I'll meet you at the hospital. Call me when you're here."

Upon my arrival at the hospital, Dad greeted me in the lobby. He didn't explain why we were here or what the emergency was. Dad led me to a room on the third level. Floor-to-ceiling glass windows allowed us to look out over the lush grass and foliage of the courtyard outside. Inside, the blue leather chairs that lined the walls of the room were occupied by Sardara Chacha Ji, Sukhi Chachi Ji, Kulwinder Massi Ji, Bachittar Massar Ji, and a few other aunties and uncles, their eyes all bearing worry.

"What's going on?" I asked. This looked serious.

Dad explained that he was about to go through the security check at the airport when he called Chacha Ji to see how Dhadhi Ji was doing. Dhadhi Ji had been dealing with ascites in her liver for the past few years and it caused her stomach to fill up with fluid. We had to take her to the hospital regularly to get it drained out, and her hospital stays were becoming longer and more frequent. She had returned home from hospital just a few days before Dad was scheduled to fly to Punjab for Baba Ji's funeral.

When Dad called from the airport, Chacha Ji had told him that Dhadhi Ji was doing okay, but that she couldn't come to the phone. When they concluded their call, Dad had the nagging sense that there was something hidden in Chacha Ji's voice, that there was something that wasn't being communicated. Dad called him back and asked to be picked up from the airport and taken to Chacha Ji's house right away. When Dad got there, paramedics were loading Dhadhi Ji into an ambulance. She had had a severe heart attack. Chacha Ji explained that in their prior phone call, he was just trying to protect Dad. He knew Dad was already going to a funeral and dealing with loss; he didn't want to burden Dad with any more grief.

A doctor wearing glasses with square-shaped lenses and his hands stuffed in the pockets of his white lab coat emerged from a dark hallway in the corner of the room. Dad and Chacha Ji both rose to greet him. The doctor explained that Dhadhi Ji's condition didn't look promising.

"Now, we have a few options," the doctor described. "We can operate, but surgery won't offer a guarantee of survival. Quality of life, continued care within the home—these are all things you'll need to consider if we choose to go this route. The other option is you can decide whether you want to let her go. To let her pass."

The doctor retreated down the hallway. We all instinctually followed. He stopped at a window outlined by a powder blue frame. I peeked over the heads of the aunties and uncles in front of me to look inside. Behind the glass, Dhadhi Ji was laying on a bed with a white sheet pulled up to her waist. Her chest slowly rose and fell as the tubes and pumps attached to her kept her breathing. Dad gave Chacha Ji a look that read we have to let her go.

Doctors declared Dhadhi Ji dead at the peak of sunset. Yellow sunbeams poured in through the windows of the waiting room. I leaned my forehead against the calming cool of the glass and pulled my cell phone out of my back pocket to call my sister Vijay.

"Hey, what's up?" she answered. I heard her daughters playing in the background. They sounded like they were all still at home. Given how quickly things had unfolded, I don't think anyone called her to tell her what was going on. I tried to speak, but the air wouldn't leave my throat.

"Amrit, are you okay?" Vijay asked.

The sun was too bright. I closed my eyes. The only words I had the strength to say out loud were "she's gone."

***

Dhadhi Ji's funeral was arranged for the morning of June 15, 2013. Dad asked me to do a speech as part of the ceremony. I was apprehensive to do it at first. I didn't think it was possible to manipulate ink and language in such a way that would adequately convey the heart of who my grandmother was and what she meant to us all. The more I sat with my speech, the best metaphor I could find to describe her life and death was an everyday colloquial Punjabi expression. At the time of someone's passing, we refer to them as becoming poora, or complete. It was a simple phrase that I had heard my parents say many times throughout my life when referring to other people who had died. I considered it to be a euphemism for death. Leading up to my grandmother's funeral though, it was the first time the meaning behind the phrase made sense. Dhadhi Ji had done all that she came on earth to do; her life's work was complete. There was nothing more left for her here.

The funeral home was packed with hundreds of people who came to pay their final respects to my grandmother. When I stood in front of them to recite my speech, in the crowd, I noticed Dad wiping tears from his eyes. It was the first time I had ever seen him cry. In the days between Dhadhi Ji's death and funeral, Dad had taken on the mantle as the face of the family, fielding phone calls from relatives and well-wishers locally and overseas, and making arrangements with the funeral home and the gurudwara. People came by the house around the clock to grieve with us. We served them with tea and food. Dad wasn't given a spare moment to lay his armour down and be alone with his thoughts—to feel, and not be a shoulder for someone else—until I was up there doing my speech.

Before we cremated my grandmother, the last person to approach her casket was Dhadha Ji. By the summer of 2013, he had spent over a year confined to a wheelchair and was dependent on others to bathe, eat, and go to the bathroom. His once strong limbs were now thinning, rigid, and always cold. His memory was betraying him as well. He'd often ask the same question multiple times in the span of a few minutes, like when he last ate, or where my father was.

I wheeled Dhadha Ji to the casket. Dad and I each hooked one of Dhadha Ji's arms and lifted him to his feet. The three of us looked down at Dhadhi Ji who lay with her hands folded over her chest, her coffin now a pool of pink and yellow flower petals. Dhadha Ji leaned forward and placed his ribs and heart against the casket. He bowed his head and put his hands together in prayer before his knees began to wobble. Hoarse and airy sobs escaped his shaking chest. Tears travelled down his cheeks and disappeared into his snow-white beard. Dad and I gently guided him back down to his wheelchair and moved him aside to clear enough space to take the casket away.

***

When Dad had explained to me that Dhadha Ji used to disappear on him for hours at a time back when they still lived in Nawan Pind, it made sense because Dhadha Ji did the same thing when I was younger.

When I was in elementary school, I'd often share the table with Dhadha Ji as I ate breakfast and watched cartoons, and he sipped his morning tea. When we parted, I'd head one way to walk to school, and he'd go the opposite direction towards the bus stop. His days were spent bussing and walking around town to wherever his whims desired, usually dividing time between the gurudwara, mall, and community centre. Sometimes I'd go for bike rides after school and find him with his friends at a park playing cards on a picnic table, each man packing his own steel thermos full of tea to help get through the day. Other times he'd bring one of his mates over to the house to meet the family. Many of his friends were widowers. The sense of community they developed kept them away from the loneliness and rumination that came from their solitude.

Even though my grandfather and I tended to leave home around the same time in the mornings, he usually returned when it was dark outside. Dhadha Ji was fiercely protective of his independence and didn't like when people asked him how he spent his day. As he aged though, continuing to stick to his routine and being unwilling to surrender some of his autonomy became more of a challenge. He could no longer remember the bus schedule that he had taken every day for years. Sometimes when he got on a bus, he couldn't recognize where his stop was and wound up staying on until he reached the end of the line. He didn't have a cell phone so when he didn't come home by dinnertime, we called his friends or the police to find out if anyone had seen him.

Despite the way his mind was wearing down, my grandfather was still physically strong, and he regularly walked the half-hour trek from home to the local gurudwara. In the winter of 2011, as was typical for my grandparents, the snowbirds left for Punjab just as the temperature in Canada was starting to drop. They wouldn't return until spring bloomed the following year. At the time of my grandparents' homecoming in April 2012, Dhadha Ji's mental and physical faculties had both abandoned him. When I had seen the condition he was in—laying supine with his glazed eyes wide open and fixated on the ceiling, unable to will enough strength to pull himself up to a seated position—I didn't understand how things could have changed so drastically. He left Canada physically fit, though with a faulty memory; he returned home just a few months later unable to take care of himself at all.

My grandparents shared a bedroom at Sardara Chacha Ji's house, their twin beds standing parallel to each other. Visiting my grandfather in the aftermath of my grandmother's death showed me a ghostliness that exists after one has passed away. Dhadhi Ji's glasses still rested on the headboard next to her gutka, which now went unopened and unread.

Her folded blanket still sat at the foot of her bed as if it anticipated her embrace. Her clothes were still neatly folded in the dresser, the only way we could remember what she smelled like. Now that my grandfather was confined to his bed and unable to move, seeing the vestiges of Dhadhi Ji's life all around him served as a constant reminder that he was alone. Dhadha Ji felt like he had stayed on this earth longer than he should have, past the point when he felt his life was complete.

***

Dhadha Ji died in his sleep in February 2014. People grieve in different ways. Many family members were distraught, crying, or withdrawn. I had two dreams about my grandfather around the time of his death that informed the way I viewed and responded to his passing. They felt more like visions than dreams.

The first one came to me the night he died, but it came before any other family members were aware of his passing. In the dream, I was playing with my nieces. They chased after a bouncing ball and I followed them to make sure they stayed safe and out of trouble. When we entered the room where the ball had diverted to, we found a framed picture of my grandfather looking just as young and healthy as he did in 1987 when he first arrived in Canada. When I woke up from the dream, Dad told me that Dhadha Ji had died. I was unfazed though. I didn't feel any distress or disturbance. Because of the dream, I felt like I already knew that he was gone.

The second vision came the night before my grandfather's funeral. Dhadha Ji was standing in front of crops and tall trees, and was surrounded by streams and bodies of water. His face looked full again, like it did before he got sick. He didn't speak in the dream, but I woke up feeling like he came to me in the vision as if to say I'm okay. Let me go. The funeral went by and I felt light, calm. There wasn't that same sadness that I had felt when my grandmother died. I felt like there was nothing left for Dhadha Ji here with us anymore, and I made my peace with it. It was in that moment that I felt like I had gained some understanding of what it meant to be unattached to this world. I was able to remove the desperation and fear that accompanied the inevitability of death. My life continued despite the people I lost along the way; to honour the memories of those I loved, I had to carry on living.

Whatever happens with Mom and her illness, whenever she is complete, I hope that I'm able to let her go as calmly as I did Dhadha Ji. Maybe that meteor shower I saw on the beach after Mom's cancer diagnosis was the vision I needed to help me prepare. Like a shooting star, we enter this world as a speck of dust in relation to the grand scale of the universe. We burn and shine briefly yet brightly; not everyone will see us, but those who did will hopefully cherish the shared experience. We go into each meteor shower with the acceptance that the moment won't exist forever, so we understand the importance of being present and giving it the attention it deserves. Despite its brevity, the memory of the shooting star stays safely vaulted in our minds, with those who witnessed it still able to vividly recall every miniscule yet beautiful detail of the sky, the moon, and all the elements that made it possible for us to behold it. When the shooting star has passed, we don't ask the universe for its lifespan to last longer; instead, we give thanks for the light we had the gift of receiving.

***

In the spring of 2014, a few months after Dhadha Ji had died, Dad travelled with Kuldip Bhua Ji and Sardara Chacha Ji to Punjab to return their parents' ashes to Nawan Pind.

The day Dad came back home to Canada after the trip, he sat with me and Mom in the kitchen. His maroon suitcase was pressed against the leg of his chair at the head of the dinner table. Newspapers and bills that had accumulated during his time away were stacked in front of him. Dad was hungry and tired after the lengthy journey home. Mom stood by the oven at the other end of the kitchen and prepared dinner for him.

"Every time I left Nawan Pind, I used to cry," Dad said. "Even after I became a Canadian citizen, I was always sad to leave the village whenever I visited. I didn't cry this time though."

I sat at the table to Dad's right. He left long pauses between his sentences. I didn't know what to say so I just listened.

Dad looked over to me. "When I die, you don't have to worry about taking my ashes back to Nawan Pind," he said. "Canada is a good resting place for me. My home is here now."

"Me too," Mom called over her shoulder. She pulled a fresh roti off the pan and laid it on a plate. "You don't need to go through all that trouble for us. We're fine here."

Dad had lived in Canada now longer than he did in Punjab; his parents were the last people in his life who could say otherwise. The idea of home and where Dad could find it had changed. I thought about how malleable the concept of home must be for him. Maybe he didn't see home as being a physical place anymore, one that was permanent and unchanging. Economic and political policies had put an end to the idyllic farming life Dad grew up with. Migration forced him to find home in trains and buses, hotels and oceans. In those spaces, all he had were his experiences, thoughts, and promises. Perhaps home was wherever he made it for himself, and home was here now.

CHAPTER FIFTEEN

NOBODY'S COUNTRY

My parents got married in 1981 through an arranged marriage. They didn't have a say in the process once the decision was made for them. My parents' personalities clashed to the point that I sometimes wondered why anyone decided to pair them together in the first place. Dad was generally calm, quiet, and rarely raised his voice. Mom could sometimes be uncompromising and quick-tempered; if she wanted things to be a certain way, we all had to fall in line. Nani Ji had said of relationships that if one is hot, the other has to be cool. Maybe my parents were such perfect opposites that they balanced each other out.

Love in my immigrant household wasn't always displayed in the most obvious ways. My parents weren't like the couples I saw on TV who were overt in the ways they expressed love to each other. They weren't affectionate with each other like Aunt Viv and Uncle Phil on *The Fresh Prince of Bel-Air*, or Homer and Marge on *The Simpsons*. My parents didn't say they loved each other, and didn't ever tell me and my sister they loved us the way Danny Tanner told his kids at the end of every *Full House* episode. Growing up, there were times when I craved just a simple acknowledgement that my parents were proud of me, that they approved of who I was and felt I was good enough, but it never came. It took me a long time to understand that it wasn't fair for me to expect a form of love from my parents that they themselves didn't receive. Dad's father was abusive and drank a lot, and Mom's father was a teacher who ran the household in the same strict fashion he did the classroom; my parents raised me as best they could with what was modelled to them.

Even though my parents weren't loving in a way that was easy for me to understand based on what the West told me love was supposed to look like, they still showed love through their actions. Mom picked out Dad's clothes for work, usually a pair of dress pants and a half-sleeved button-up shirt, that she ironed and laid on the edge of the bed for him every night. When I was still in elementary school, if Mom had to work early in the morning, she made sure to comb my hair and tie a joora atop my head before I went to bed the night prior. I'd make her do it over again until I felt it was tight and sturdy enough to endure the games of soccer and hockey I would play with my friends during recess. When Mom was working late, she left handwritten notes instructing us where we could find easily microwavable meals after school. As I grew older, I saw that love between my parents wasn't shared through words but exemplified in the way they followed each other from Punjab to Canada to start a new life together. Love was seen in the way Dad made himself present for Mom during times of ill health, and how he massaged her aching shoulders every evening. As I grew up and started to understand that these actions are synonyms for love, it helped me understand that we all give love, and are loved, more than we can ever know.

My parents' celebrated their 36th wedding anniversary on December 5, 2017. Mom only had a few weeks of chemo and radiation treatment remaining. We celebrated with a mousse cake, which was the only solid food that was soft enough for Mom to chew. Since the surgery, she had survived on a diet of protein shakes, oatmeal, and dhaal; she could use the cake and a bit of sweetness to awaken her taste buds. After dinner, Nuvi and I were washing dishes when we heard Mom raise her voice upstairs. I couldn't make out her words but she sounded upset.

"No, I don't want to go." Mom's voice grew clearer as I ascended the stairs. She sat on the edge of her bed wearing red and black plaid pajamas, and an orange bandana over her head. The collar of her top kept sliding down her sloping left shoulder.

"We have to be safe," Dad responded. His eyebrows were raised in concern. He knelt on the floor in front of Mom, his right hand placed over her left. He was still dressed in his work clothes—brown pants and a powder blue shirt, with a royal blue dastaar. Mom refused to look him in the eyes and stared past him towards the TV where CP24 endlessly scrolled through the day's headlines.

"What's going on?" I asked, leaning against the doorframe.

"I'm fine," Mom said. She wrestled her hand free of Dad's.

"The doctor told us today that if your mom ever gets a fever while she's still going through radiation, we have to take her to the emergency room," Dad explained. He sighed and rose to his feet.

"Let me stay home tonight," said Mom. "If I still have a fever in the morning, I'll go to the ER then."

"We shouldn't take any chances with this," Dad pleaded.

He looked over towards me and paused for a moment. It felt like he wanted me to back him up and tell Mom that we needed to go to the hospital. The winds moaned with a high-pitched howl over the sound of the television and slammed against the window. Mom had already gone to Sunnybrook for radiation treatment earlier in the day, I thought; I could understand why she didn't want to leave home again in this cold to spend even more time in a hospital. I understood Dad's concerns too though; we had to take the doctor's warnings seriously.

"Come on," Dad said, making the decision for all of us. "Let's go." Dad helped Mom up to her feet. I packed her medications, toiletries, and a change of clothes in a plastic bag.

Mom, Dad, Nuvi, and I arrived at Brampton Civic Hospital at 10:00 p.m. It was a busy night in the ER. Nurses rushed patients on stretchers past us. Police spoke to a man who was laying across a few chairs and looked to be intoxicated. Concerned parents sat with crying babies in their laps. An elderly couple sat next to us holding hands. I wondered if it was their anniversary too. By midnight, Mom still hadn't been seen by a doctor. I told Dad to go home so he could rest, and that Nuvi and I would wait here with Mom.

"Call me if anything happens," Dad said. He lifted his beard to pull the zipper on his winter coat all the way up. "I'll have my phone by my bed."

When Mom was finally seen by a doctor that night, the worry was that she had developed cellulitis in the skin where the radiation therapy was being focused. The doctor prescribed Mom antibiotics. We didn't leave the hospital until close to 3:00 a.m. Dad was fast asleep by the time we got home. I thought about waking him to let him know we were back, but decided he needed his rest. Mom did too. It could wait until morning.

***

A few days later, Mom, Dad, and I drove back home from Sunnybrook Hospital. I had the day off from work and was scheduled to take Mom to her appointments that afternoon, but on longer days when she had both radiation and chemotherapy scheduled one after the other, she preferred to have Dad by her side. I decided to tag along with them so they wouldn't have to go through the whole day alone.

Dad had been able to maintain his flexed schedule for much of October, but as Mom's treatment carried on into November and December, he missed a few days of work to fit in her growing number of appointments. It wasn't like him to miss work. We still didn't know for sure how Mom was progressing with her treatment, but the fever she had on their anniversary had subsided and her temperature had been steady since then. The antibiotics proved to be effective as her cellulitis was healing as well—all positive signs that I classified as progress. To get a better understanding of whether the chemo and radiation were working though, we had to keep holding our collective breath until April when Mom would see Dr. Higgins again. The worst part was waiting and trying to go about life every day with a giant question mark hanging over our heads. All that we could do now was try to make Mom comfortable.

Toronto traffic was perpetually in rush hour. A red sea of brake lights surrounded us and delayed us in our return journey home from the hospital. Mom sat in the passenger seat and was in a great deal of pain. She was on the verge of tears and stomped her feet against the car mats. She begged us to get home as quickly as possible. Dad and I were both silent; there was nothing that we could do but wait for the traffic to clear up. Eventually, Mom fell asleep with her head leaned against the car window. She had pulled the hood of her coat up to protect herself against the coldness of the glass. Her breath condensed and evaporated on the window with each exhale and inhale.

We made it home from Sunnybrook that evening just after 7:00 p.m. Mom went upstairs to her room to prepare for bed. She liked to watch her shows at night, the ones that she had recorded on the PVR when she was at the hospital for treatment. She mostly watched Indian soap operas and singing competitions. Mom would clap in appreciation when she heard a singer that she really liked. It was one of the few things in life now that made her happy and helped her forget about the pain she was in.

As Mom settled into her nighttime routine, Dad was in the kitchen making warm milk for himself and Mom to drink. He was ready for bed too, having removed his dastaar and changed into his white kurtha. Deep wrinkles followed crooked paths across his forehead. Dad tilted a milk bag into a metal pot and turned on the stove. The gas lighter clicked four times before blue and orange flames emanated from the burner. I crushed fennel seeds and cardamom with a steel mortar and pestle and poured the remnants into the milk.

"After Jasvir's wedding, I was back in the village for about two months," Dad explained. "I stayed over at Raj's house a lot during that time. His village was bigger and had more bus service. I took the bus from Bidhipur down GT Road to his place. After staying there for a week or two, he'd come back with me to stay in Nawan Pind for a bit. We got along really well with each other's families. Sometimes my siblings would come to his house with me and spend the night—that's how comfortable we all felt with each other."

"I always had the thought that you worked on the ships for a longer period of time," I said. "You weren't even gone for two years though."

"That was the first time I went out. It wasn't the last time."

During their time off after Jasvir's wedding, Dad explained that he and Raj had strategized on how they would get back to work in Europe later that summer. They had made good money in the time they were away from home, and wanted to set themselves up for long-term financial stability by becoming citizens somewhere in Europe.

"We thought maybe we could apply for citizenship in Greece because we had worked for a Greek shipping company," Dad noted. "I liked the Greek people, the food. I knew some of the language. The problem was that most of our work didn't actually take place in Greece." Dad pulled out two blue teacups from the cupboard above the stove and set them down on the marble countertop. "Even though the company I worked for was Greek, when you work on the oceans, you can't claim that as work you've done in Greece. You can't use that experience to make a case for why you want to be in a certain country. Out on the water, it's nobody's country."

"Is that when you started thinking about coming to Canada?" I asked.

"No," Dad shook his head. "Raj had a brother-in-law who lived in Holland. If I remember right, I think he was in the city of Utrecht. Raj suggested that we visit him to see what the process was to become

Dutch citizens. We weren't sure how we would get to the Netherlands though." A smile started to build on Dad's face. "There was one guy from Raj's village who said he could help us. He said that he had family in the Netherlands who had connections with the immigration department there, and all that he had to do was make a few phone calls and he could get us in. He said he could provide us with letters that would easily get us approved for visas. We asked him to get the letters for us and he did." Dad interrupted his story to laugh to himself. "So, he brings us the letters, and Raj and I take them to Delhi to apply for visas to visit Holland. We gave the letters to the person working at the immigration office, and we could tell that she was suspicious of us. She asked if we had the envelopes the letters came in. We were never given envelopes so we lied and said we threw them in the trash. The lady called her manager over. When he looked at the letters, he yelled at us and said they were fake. He threw them back in our faces and told us to get out of his office. We ran out of there as fast we could. When we got back to the village, Raj found that guy who gave us the letters and slapped him so hard."

Though Dad could find humour in the situation in hindsight, the scenario painted an image in my mind that there was a growing group of conmen and hustlers who were looking to make a dollar on the pervading sense of desperation throughout Punjab. In the changing economic landscape, people needed money and jobs to survive; many felt they needed to get out of the country to find other opportunities, but were falling prey to smugglers and other scam artists who were looking to capitalize. Dad said he and Raj couldn't show their faces in the immigration office in Delhi again after what had happened with the phony letters. Instead, they found other ways to leave India.

"Raj and I had some money now, so we didn't have to travel by land," Dad explained. "We could afford to fly to wherever we wanted to go. People with Indian citizenship didn't need a visa to travel to Nepal, so instead of trying to go through Afghanistan again, we decided to go to Kathmandu first."

Dad and I leaned against the countertops on either side of the stove. He swirled a spoon in the milk that scratched against the bottom of the pot. Dad said he didn't expect to see so many white Americans in Kathmandu. Many of them flocked to the popular tourist area known as Freak Street to smoke weed and buy legal hashish from government-run shops. While in Nepal, Dad and Raj obtained tourist visas from the Royal Thai Embassy on August 24, 1977 and arranged to fly to Bangkok the next day. In Thailand, they got their tourist visas to travel to Poland, which was their first European destination on route to the Netherlands.

"Before we left Bangkok, something told me we should apply for tourist visas to Greece," Dad said. "Citizenship in the Netherlands was our goal, but we still thought we should try to get visas for Greece as a backup plan just in case things didn't pan out for us and we decided to work on the ships again." He and Raj were granted visas from the Greek embassy in Thailand on August 29, 1977.

Dad and Raj had to create new travel plans in each country they landed in. For every city, they would find train and ferry schedules, and they moved using the most cost-efficient routes to get from place to place, simultaneously building a bridge while crossing it. From Warsaw, Poland, Raj and Dad travelled via train to Denmark and found lodgings in a youth hostel. They reacclimatized themselves to life on the waters by boarding a ferry that took them from Denmark to Amsterdam. Raj's brother-in-law greeted them there and took them to his home in Utrecht.

Bubbles started to form in the milk. Dad pulled the pot off the flames. He let the froth subside before putting the pot over the fire a second time. He waited for the milk to reach its boiling point again.

"We had no money in hand, no fixed destination, and no papers," Dad said. He shook his head as if he finally realized the dangers of the situation he had put himself in. "We had a loose plan, but we were really just travelling from country to country and looking for work. God helps though."

***

Satnam and Raj sat on the beach. White sands, warm sunlight that flowed down through a cloudless sky, cliffs that hung over turquoise waters. It was September 1977. Satnam was twenty-three years old.

"This is where I want to stay," Satnam said.

He hadn't seen water this clear, this blue. Working aboard the ships, the seas looked murky and grey the further out from land he got. From here, he could see deep below the surface, like the waters had nothing to hide.

"We can't stay here, you know that," said Raj. They both kept their eyes on the water, smooth as glass as it moved.

"I know." Satnam broke eye contact with the sea and looked down, fixating on the sand between his feet. "It would have been nice to stay here is all I meant. To be a citizen."

They were in Crete, a popular vacation destination in the Greek islands. The Netherlands didn't pan out for them as a spot where they could become citizens.

When they had arrived in Utrecht a few weeks prior to returning to Greece, Raj's brother-in-law Arun had explained that there were plenty of steady jobs there, and that foreigners mainly found work in factories, restaurants, or farms. However, the process of becoming citizens was complicated. Arun informed Satnam and Raj about one option that he had seen some people use to gain Dutch citizenship that involved women from Suriname. As citizens of the South American nation that was a former Dutch colony, Surinamese people could freely enter the Netherlands without needing a visa. For a fee, there were underworld agents who would arrange a sham marriage between a Surinamese woman and whoever was looking to settle in the Netherlands. Satnam told Arun that that he couldn't go through with that idea; he had just been back home in Nawan Pind for his sister Jasvir's wedding, and saw how important marriage was to his family; Satnam couldn't live with his conscience if he went through with a fake one, even if it was only temporary.

Before Satnam and Raj left the Netherlands, Arun had suggested they speak to a friend of his who was an immigration lawyer in West Germany. Arun drove Satnam and Raj over the border for the meeting, and the lawyer advised that Satnam use his religion to anchor himself in Europe. Thousands of Sikh men throughout the seventies had been applying for political asylum in countries like West Germany, Belgium, and France due to the worsening political climate in India.

In 1971, Indira Gandhi had defeated Raj Narain to become India's Prime Minister. Narain appealed the decision with the High Court and on June 12, 1975, Gandhi was found guilty of having committed election fraud. Her victory was considered invalid and the High Court barred her from holding office. Gandhi's Congress Party was given twenty days to choose another leader to replace her as Prime Minister. Gandhi decided to contest the verdict in the Supreme Court. On June 24, 1975, the Supreme Court granted her a partial stay, noting that until the appeal was resolved, Gandhi could remain a member of parliament, though her right to vote in parliamentary matters was revoked.

In 1974 and 1975, prior to the confirmation of election fraud, anti-Gandhi protests had flared across India in places like Gujarat and Bihar around matters of food scarcity, surging food prices, corruption, and widespread unemployment. A massive political rally calling for Gandhi's immediate resignation was held in Delhi the day after the Supreme Court's ruling. In a move designed to protect herself and her power, Gandhi had urged Indian president Fakhruddin Ali Ahmed to declare a state of emergency over fears that the rallies and protests would threaten the security of the nation. Three hours after Ahmed announced the state of emergency, Gandhi cut off electricity to all major newspapers and created a media blackout. Anyone who spoke out against her was detained. India's democracy started to resemble a dictatorship as the state of emergency gave Gandhi greater powers than what the Indian constitution normally permitted a leader to have.

The state of emergency ended nearly two years later in March 1977 with 140 000 people—including 60 000 Sikhs—having been arrested, held without trial, and thrown in jail. Violence committed by the Indian state as a form of suppression against peaceful protest became more commonplace. Many Sikhs who had left India for political asylum found safety in Europe. The unrest was real; those who fled couldn't go back home.

While Satnam and Raj were still in West Germany, the lawyer had explained to them that applying for political asylum wasn't a guarantee that they would be allowed to stay. However, he still advised them to apply because they could remain in the country for as long as it took the state to process their applications. In that time, Satnam and Raj could still find jobs and earn money. If their stays were approved, they'd have a new place to call home. If they were denied though, they would be deported back to India. Satnam thanked the lawyer for his advice but turned down the offer. He didn't want to use the pain of other Sikhs for his own benefit.

Feeling that they had nowhere else to go, Satnam and Raj decided to use the tourist visas they got back in Thailand and made plans to return to Greece. To ward off any suspicions that they weren't actually tourists, they booked vacation packages for Crete and planned to stay there for a few days as a decoy before leaving the island to find work in the shipyards in Piraeus.

Maybe citizenship somewhere in Europe wasn't in the cards for them—at least, not right now. Greece may not have been where they wanted to go when they had initially left Punjab this time around, but at least they could make money doing jobs they enjoyed.

Between talking to lawyers and arranging their travel to Greece, Satnam and Raj had spent two weeks in the Netherlands and West Germany. During that time, they discovered an underground world of migrant South Asian workers. Some of them were well paid and lived in flats they rented close to the factories that employed them; others struggled to get by. Those who were being paid lower wages or were still having their political asylum applications processed by the West German government often bunked in motels with more than five people in each room. The demanding physical labour jobs combined with the looming threat of deportation made nightfall around these motels chaotic. Satnam had witnessed heated arguments between Indians and Pakistanis turn into fistfights fueled by alcohol and patriotism. Thrust into competition with each other for work, their paranoia around when they would be deported caused them to lash out violently.

"Okay, so the Netherlands didn't work out like we thought it would," Raj said to Satnam, still staring out at the horizon where sea met sky. "It's frustrating for me too. But we have homes already back in Punjab. Don't forget about that when you're chasing something out here. Greece is just for now. We won't be running forever."

Satnam grabbed a handful of white sand and let it pour through his fingers like an hourglass. "This money we make on the ship won't last for a long time. Citizenship would have solved all that. Sometimes I feel like running is all I know how to do."

"Come on, don't think like that," Raj said. "This isn't the end. We won't be running like this for the rest of our lives. With any luck, we can settle down and be back here in Greece someday as citizens."

Satnam rose to his feet and dug his toes into the sand one last time. He appreciated Raj's eternal optimism. Satnam turned away from the waters and started walking back towards the hotel. "Someday."

SINKING

In Piraeus, Raj and Satnam used an employment agency to find work, and they were arranged to join a crew led by a captain named Alex. A few months into their second tenure on the waters, stormy conditions descended upon the Bay of Biscay as their ship travelled from France to Spain for a delivery. Swift and powerful winds jostled the ship back and forth. Alex watched from the bridge and stood next to Satnam who steered the vessel. Satnam's reputation for being an excellent wheelman had followed him to his new job and he spent most of his shifts at the helm.

"Do you hear that?" Alex asked.

Satnam paused to listen. "It just sounds like rain to me."

"No, listen close."

Both men stopped moving to pay closer attention. Through a pause in the rain, Alex noticed something outside the window. The tarp cover tied over one of the ship's hatchways had become undone and was flailing in the wind. Rain poured in and soaked the cargo below the deck's surface. More pressingly though, Alex was concerned that the tarp could get caught in one of the ship's propellers and compromise the safety of the entire crew on board.

"What do we do?" Satnam asked.

Alex picked his jacket up from the hook on the back of the door. "The first officer will have to steer," he said. Alex shoved his arms through the sleeves of his jacket and pulled the zipper up to his chin. "Satnam, I need you to come with me to secure the tarp."

Alex led the way downstairs from the bridge to the ship's deck. At the bottom of the staircase, they ran into two other sailors.

"You two come with me," Alex commanded. "We need your help right now."

Satnam pulled the hood of his raincoat over his head and held his breath to brace himself for the storm.

The wind and the waves staggered the group of four and made it hard for them to find steady footing. The tarp had become slick with rainwater and was difficult to hold and tie down. Satnam heard Alex's voice shouting instructions, but couldn't make out the contents of his message over the sounds of the rain pattering on their hoods and the tarp whipping against the wind.

A large wave crashed aboard the deck. The impact of the wave tilted the ship over to one side and swept all four men off their feet. Gravity and momentum sent Satnam sliding towards the edge of the ship. He slid feet-first on his back along the deck's surface. He flailed his arms out to grab hold of anything that would slow his descent. Flashes of wood and steel. Panic. All supports were just outside of his grasp. Trying to grab the steel railing that outlined the perimeter of the deck would be his last hope to save himself from going overboard.

Satnam's feet slid under the rail. He extended his arms up, and his elbows locked around the steel. With his back pressed to the deck, Satnam's legs dangled over the edge of the ship. Waves lunged up and bit at his heels. The ship steadied itself back to an upright position.

"I'm over here!" Satnam shouted, struggling to catch his breath.

Alex and the other two sailors climbed to their feet and ran to where Satnam still held on to the railing. The three of them pulled him back aboard.

"We almost lost you there," Alex said. He helped Satnam up to a standing position.

Satnam breathed in deeply and exhaled. "Almost."

***

From Spain, the crew went on to deliver a shipment of goods to Romania. They then travelled to Russia to load up on a cargo of cement to be delivered at Shuwaikh Port in Kuwait. Due to a delay in the receiving end of the port, ships were lined up for miles with their anchors dropped while waiting for their turn to approach land. Satnam's ship spent nearly a month off the coast of Kuwait before his team could unload their cargo. Work slowed to a halt.

One afternoon, while still waiting outside Shuwaikh Port, Satnam and Raj sat on the deck of their ship playing cards. Suddenly, a brown cloud rose up from the land and floated out towards the water. The plume kept growing in speed and size. It rose high enough to steal the sun from the sky and forced the city into darkness.

All the sailors ran inside their quarters for refuge from the dust and debris being whipped at them. The sandstorm wouldn't relent. Covering his mouth with a handkerchief, Satnam still swallowed grains of sand down with every breath he took. Visibility both inside the ship and out became limited. The once bright and sunny day in Kuwait quickly became enveloped in blackness.

The storm subsided an hour later. When the air cleared, the crew found that every surface of their freighter was buried under inches of sand. All the other ships lined up along the port were similarly blanketed, looking like they were camouflaged for desert warfare.

From Kuwait, Satnam's vessel sailed to Manama, Bahrain. The heat there was unlike anything he had felt anywhere else in the world. Even in the mornings, when the sun hadn't fully risen to erase the night from the sky, it would already be so hot that the entire crew was soaked with sweat and working in their t-shirts and boxers in failed attempts to stay cool.

In the afternoon of their second day in Bahrain, a few crewmembers working out on the deck noticed smoke coming from the engine room. Some of them grabbed fire extinguishers, but they were cut off by Raj running in the opposite direction.

"Fire!" Raj shouted. He told the other men that the flames in the engine room had swelled too big for extinguishers now, and that Captain Alex had to be notified.

Alex sent out SOS signals to the port authority in Manama and ordered the entire crew to abandon ship immediately. There was no time for anyone to change clothes or grab their belongings. Readying the emergency rafts, all crewmembers got off the ship and scattered themselves at a safe distance from the burning vessel. Help from the port arrived an hour later. All crew were taken to the mainland where they were put up in hotels until an investigation by their insurance company could be completed to determine the cause of the fire and the extent of the damage. By the time Satnam and Raj were processed by Bahraini immigration officials and settled in their hotel rooms, they had gone over twenty-four hours without food, water, or sleep.

The insurance company's investigation concluded that the ship wasn't deliberately set on fire, though the damage was bad enough that the freighter needed to be scrapped. All the electrical wiring aboard was fried. Glass windows had exploded from the heat. Parts of the ship's wood and steel supports had been torched. The fire didn't damage the entirety of the ship though, and the crew were eventually allowed to climb back aboard to collect their items from their quarters. Alex gathered his crew in the lobby of the hotel and informed them that word had come from their head office that everyone would have their full wages for this delivery paid, but they would all be sent home. For the Greek nationals on the crew, they weren't too bothered by the news as they would be able to get back to work after a few weeks of rest at home. For Satnam and Raj though, it wasn't that simple. All the border hopping they did through Nepal, Thailand, Poland, Denmark, the Netherlands, and West Germany to make it back to Greece this time around felt like it was for nothing since they were being sent back home again after just a few months.

As the two friends boarded their flight back to Delhi from Bahrain, they didn't know what their futures held. They were supposed to be the financial saviours of their families, but they were now out of jobs and didn't know how or when they would get back into a position where they could earn again.

***

When I think about my relationship with my father, about how we became so quiet and distant from each other, it was more of a gradual drifting apart than a dramatic blow-up. The family trip to Punjab in 1993 was a pivotal time that marked a shift in how we communicated with each other. Before then, love between us seemed to be easily understood. Dad played baseball with me in the backyard on weekends. One of the trees in the garden was first base, the backdoor to the house was second base, and the clothes rack was third. He pitched soft and under-handed so I always made contact. One morning, he surprised me with a Montreal

Expos bat and ball. I was so excited that I ran out to the backyard so we could play before we even had breakfast. My favourite outings with him were our trips to the library. I picked out a new book—*Little Critters* or *Barenstein Bears* or *Tyrone the Terrible*—and Dad would read to me every night before bed. He used animated voices to represent each of the different characters.

On summer nights, Mom, Dad, Vijay, and I would ride our bikes as a family to different parks in Malton. Dad would push me on the swings until the earth disappeared beneath me, and the sight of my outstretched sneakers kicking towards the dimming purple and navy blue of the evening sky was the only thing I saw. As I got older though, I felt like Dad's lighthearted side was gone and he had more demands of me. The constant pressure that he put on me to be an exceptional student was hard for me to exist under. My success was seen more as an expectation and not an achievement. In the exchange of immigration, he saw himself as part of the generation that sacrificed, and I belonged to the generation that needed to actualize. There was no time for me to fail or be average at things he needed me to excel at like math, science, and English; there was no space for me to try things out like art and music that he considered to be unfeasible or unrealistic as career paths. It made me feel like who I was as a person and the things that mattered to me weren't ever good enough for him. However, what I didn't realize at the time was that in the mid-nineties, when Dad became solely focused on my success, he was going through his own struggles: he had grown disillusioned with the Canadian dream that was sold to him.

After arriving in Canada in 1982 at age twenty-eight, Dad had initially applied to Humber College in Rexdale to become a welder. Shortly after starting his studies, he changed focus and enrolled himself in Sheridan College's architectural drafting program. While at Sheridan, he got his first job in Canada at a factory that mass-produced furniture for stores like The Bay and Sears. Working on the loading dock, Dad moved furniture onto trucks for shipping, and travelled by bus to get to college in between shifts at the factory.

Dad looked to his uncles Bachittar and Harbhajan to impart knowledge on how to get ahead in Canada as the two of them had been in the West for over a decade by the time Dad joined them. They had worked long hours at physically demanding labour jobs and felt that the only way to make any progress here was to own something for themselves.

Harbhajan and Bachittar pooled their resources to start their own furniture company together. The idea for the business came when Dad had tried reupholstering an old couch at the house they all lived in. Impressed with his own handiwork, Dad dropped out of college after one semester to help run the family business with his uncles. The three of them christened their venture with the name Custom Upholstery.

By the summer of 1983, Mom gave birth to my sister Vijay. Soon after that, my parents purchased their first home in Brampton. Balancing a new baby, a new home, and a new business, Dad's day typically started long before sunrise. He would begin by dropping Vijay off at Amarjit Mamma Ji's house in Malton to be babysat by Nani Ji and Nana Ji, before driving Mom to her job in Mississauga. From there, Dad clocked in eight hours at his day job in North York where he manufactured furniture for an Italian-owned company. After work, he rushed through traffic to pick up both Vijay and Mom and dropped them back to the family home in Brampton. He then went to the newly-leased Custom Upholstery warehouse in Mississauga where he worked until 11:00 p.m. every night. The next day, Dad repeated the cycle all over again.

Weekends were a bit calmer as Dad spent full days working with his uncles rather than dividing his time between two jobs, but the schedule had taken a toll on his life at home. Mom was spending evenings and weekends alone with Vijay, and felt deserted in her own home without a partner to help raise their child. When Dad would finish work and return home late at night, he memorized the number of steps it would take to travel through the house in the dark without turning on a light and alerting Mom and Vijay of his arrival. Hanging his sweaty and rumpled clothes in the closet before crawling into bed, Mom still woke up every time and asked him how long he would continue to put himself through this. Dad told me that he didn't earn a dollar from the business in the years he spent working there.

When we returned to Canada from the trip to Nawan Pind in 1993, Dad was ready to pack up the family and go back to Punjab permanently. By that point, he had been in Canada for over ten years; he decided that the West wasn't what he thought it would be. It felt like those weeks we had spent back in the village reminded Dad of everything he had given up, everything he had lost. He had been working hard in Canada and was able to afford a middle-class lifestyle, but the financial freedom that he was told his labour was supposed to return—the promise of the

West that in part influenced why he left his village in Punjab all those years ago—still eluded him. Dad told Mom, Vijay, and me to pack our things. I tried to be better, hoping that if I got higher grades in school he'd reconsider. I didn't want to leave. As much as I loved Punjab while I was there, the only life I had ever known was in Canada. Bachittar Massar Ji put his foot down and told Dad that he could go back to Punjab if he wanted to, but that he couldn't take me and Vijay with him; we shouldn't be uprooted because Dad was frustrated. Dad stopped talking about moving after that. The pressure he put on me to succeed didn't subside though, and his need to control things continued.

When Dad began visiting Baba Ji daily around 1997, he asked me and Vijay to recite Japji Sahib every morning and Rehraas Sahib every evening. He followed up with us every day like he was checking homework to ensure we had said our prayers. I could see that it meant a lot to Dad so I did it, but it felt like an obligation I had to fulfill. There was nothing wrong with him asking us to learn about Sikhi and Gurbani, but there wasn't ever any discourse around Sikhi at home, about what the words meant and why they were meaningful. Gurbani wasn't treated as something to engage with, but just something that we had to do. Dad felt that because he was becoming more in tune with his spirituality that we all should be doing the same. Sikhi was what he felt saved him from the unhappiness he had experienced living in Canada, but with me, he treated religion the same way he treated school: it was another expectation, something I felt like I had to do to be a good enough son for him. To Dad, spirituality represented freedom; to me, it was obedience and submission to something I didn't understand and wasn't ever explained to me. I felt like I wasn't allowed to form my own relationship with Sikhi at my own pace. As much as Vijay and I tried to keep up with Dad's demands, we were still asked why we couldn't be like other people's kids who prayed more than we did and wore all the outward physical attributes of the Sikh identity. After a while, I stopped putting up a front. I stopped trying.

Maybe that was why Dad and I never got to know each other. Outside of spending time with him when we had to work to do, we never learned how to communicate on a personal level. He didn't share the details of his life with me, and I developed into my own person with my own goals and hobbies without ever really divulging to Dad what those interests were; I didn't want to open myself up to feeling like I wasn't good enough anymore. I still admired and respected Dad for everything he did and sacrificed for the family, but I didn't know how to disrupt that silence between us. I felt it was too late, that we would just remain what we were now as strangers who had an unspoken love for each other, but didn't ever learn how to build a relationship and connection around that love. There was a time though when I felt I could not hide anymore, when the silence was hurting me.

***

My heart felt like it was sinking.

It was the summer of 2006 and I felt a heavy, sinking feeling in my chest. I was nineteen years old. Without reason and without any sort of triggering event or experience, life changed for me. Some sensations were lost: I didn't ever feel hungry, my energy levels were depleted, and I couldn't fall asleep. My cousins from England were visiting that summer, and even though I spent every day with them, I didn't feel happiness like I usually did when I was around them. My ability to feel any joy followed my appetite, sleep, and vitality into an abyss.

Other sensations appeared that were new: my body felt heavy and uncooperative, my head felt like it was in a thick fog, and I felt a deep sadness most of the time; the rest of the time, I was numb and felt nothing. What I remember feeling most was the sinking in my chest.

My cousins recognized that I wasn't acting like my usual self. They asked me if I was okay, and I said that I was, but I didn't know what was wrong. If I couldn't find the words to explain this feeling to myself, how could I explain it to them? Whatever this feeling was, it severed my tongue and robbed me of my vocabulary. I didn't want to explain myself though—I wanted to be left alone. In my sadness, I chose to withdraw from everyone. I hoped that things would return to normal once my cousins left and I could get back to my normal routine. September and a new semester at university were right around the corner. Going back to school didn't change anything though. That sorrow, that sinking, became my new normal and I carried it with me every day.

I completed my undergraduate and graduate degrees and entered the working world, but that sinking feeling still lived in me like an unwelcome house guest that had taken up space in my body. I wasn't comfortable with it being there, but I accepted it as being my reality.

At work, there were days when I would sit in my cubicle and stare at my computer screen for hours, but couldn't will myself to do anything. My eyes couldn't focus on the words on the monitor. My head was so foggy that I had difficulty retaining new information. When I drove home on the ninety-minute commute from work every day, I struggled to concentrate on the road. I tried pinching my legs, slapping my chest—anything I could do to keep myself alert and to avoid swerving off the road.

When I got home, I'd retreat to my bed for the rest of the evening, still dressed in my work clothes. I didn't have the energy to cover myself with a blanket; I felt too heavy to move. Simple things felt overwhelming and impossible to do, like my body and mind were rebelling against each other. I wanted to disappear, but at the same time, I wanted someone to see me—to recognize that something was wrong, and to give me the language to describe myself that I didn't yet have. I didn't tell anyone what I was going through; I didn't feel like anyone would understand it. And, I reasoned, how could they? Everyone else around me—my family, friends, and coworkers—were able to go to work and get things done in life and feel joy with seemingly no difficulty. Falling victim to the sinking in my chest and letting it take hold of me the way it did made me feel that I was worthless and defective. Thoughts of self-loathing, shame, and disappearing into oblivion invaded my mind.

One day at work in 2015, my breathing suddenly became shallow. I felt like I had a knot in my throat. I got up from my desk and walked on trembling legs to the private restroom. My fingers fumbled with the doorknob but I managed to lock it behind me. I dropped to my knees in front of the toilet. I felt like I was going to vomit. I started crying—uncontrollably, deeply—from my chest. I couldn't remember the last time I cried, when I felt something other than the sinking. I got up and splashed my face with cold water. I tried to get back to work but the tears returned. There were too many to wash away. I sat back down on the floor of the bathroom with my back against the door, and tried to keep the world out so no one would see me in here like this.

I tried to control my breathing, but I couldn't get enough oxygen in. My chest heaved and shuddered from the uneven gasps of air that couldn't find their way far enough into my lungs. I sat on the floor for a few moments more. I started wondering how many minutes I'd been away from my desk. How long had it been? I thought. How long was I in here? My supervisors must be wondering where I am and why I've been gone. The only voice I heard in my head as I sat on the floor was Dad's—all the times he told me how he didn't ever call in sick or miss a day of work. He spoke with pride about how much he could do and how long he could go. It was all he knew. It became all I knew. I got up, dusted the back of my pants off, and went back to my desk.

***

Living in silence was becoming too difficult to manage. I decided that I needed to tell my father the truth about what I was going through.

One Saturday, I found Dad working in the backyard. I had just come home from an appointment with a psychologist. It was the spring of 2015. I was twenty-eight years old. Dad was preparing the garden so we could grow our own vegetables, just as we did every year. Though he couldn't farm in Punjab as a career anymore, he couldn't shake his love for farming. My parents said the vegetables grown at home tasted better than the ones we got at the grocery store, and the difference was that ours were planted with love and care.

Eight white bags of fertilizer were spread out along the garden that ran the length of the backyard. Dad wore a navy blue tracksuit and stood ankles-deep in the soil. His track bottoms were tucked into maroon boots that rose halfway up to his knees. He wore those same boots every summer when gardening and every winter when he shoveled snow. They were the first pair of winter boots he bought when he came to Canada in 1982.

The sun was high in the sky and white pillows of cloud were nudged along by a gentle breeze. Dad leaned forward and cut a hole in one of the fertilizer bags with the black, metal trowel he grasped in his gloved hand. I didn't say anything, but he noticed me standing by the wooden gate leading to the backyard.

"I was looking for you earlier," Dad said. "Can you help me out?" I swung open the gate and turned over the bag of fertilizer. "Where did you go today?" he asked. "I talked to your mom, but she wasn't really sure either."

I used a rake to evenly spread and smooth out the fertilizer until the faded brown of last year's earth blended in with the darker covering that enriched it.

156

"I wanted to talk to you about that," I said.

Dad stood upright and stepped out of the soil. He stomped his boots on the grass to shake the dirt loose.

"These last few weeks," I explained, "I've been getting some help."

"What kind of help?" Dad asked. The sweat glistened on his forehead.

"I went to see a psychologist and psychiatrist this month." I couldn't bring my eyes to meet his. "I've been dealing with depression for a while. I needed to talk to someone."

Nuvi was the one who encouraged me to reach out to a professional. She was the only person I openly talked to about what I was going through. She reasoned that if I had been dealing with this on my own for so long with no improvement, maybe it would help to talk to a doctor about it. After completing a battery of assessments with a psychologist and a psychiatrist, I was diagnosed with having major depression and generalized anxiety. I finally gained the words that I had desperately been searching for over the past nine years. The one solace I took from this malaise was that if there were words for these conditions, then I wasn't alone; there must be others who felt the same way I did.

"Depression?" Dad's eyes squinted as he spoke, like he couldn't believe the words falling out of his mouth. "What do you have to be depressed about?"

I threw the rake down. I just wanted him to hear me out, not judge me. I sat on the picnic table in the shade, hoping the darkness would hide the tears pooling in my eyes.

"I grew up poor, but we didn't ever get depressed," Dad said. He followed me over to the table. "Your mom and I, we work so hard to give you everything you could ever want, to give you the life we never had—"

"Dad, just stop. Please."

He peeled his gloves off and sat next to me. "What's wrong? Is there something that happened that's making you feel this way?"

"It's not about money. I know you and Mom do so much, and I'm grateful for all of it. It's not because of anything that happened to me. Nothing happened. I'm just depressed. I don't know how else to explain it to you."

A tear escaped my eye and fell into my lap. I felt selfish for feeling this way, for making Dad worry this much about me. I felt guilty for making him think that he, and not my own flawed brain chemistry, was somehow responsible for what I was going through.

"What can we do? How do we make this better?" Dad asked.

"I don't know," I shrugged.

I thought about whether it would be easier to drop the conversation altogether, to stay distant. I felt Dad wasn't understanding it the way I wanted him to. I wasn't unwell in a way he would recognize—I wasn't bleeding, my bones were intact, my lungs were still pumping air. In the absence of anything tangible to mourn or grieve over, I didn't know how to explain why I felt this sorrow deep in my chest. I grew up with all the luxuries and privileges that his migration was supposed to solve: water, food, electricity, shelter, education. Having all of those things and still being depressed wasn't part of his plan.

"I don't want you to make it better—I just want you to listen," I said. I raised my head and looked towards the garden. "I don't think this is something you can solve. I'm getting the help I need and working through it in my own way."

"Okay," he said. He slid an arm over my shoulders and we watched the newborn leaves dance in the wind.

Maybe I couldn't blame Dad for the fact that, up until that point, we didn't really know each other. Maybe there were other factors that I wasn't seeing. In all those years that I pulled back from the family because I needed to figure out what was going on with my mental health, I didn't consider that Dad was figuring things out for himself too. For much of my life, I only saw Dad for what he didn't give me. I didn't stop to consider what the world didn't give him. Fatherhood, earning money, running a household, being a caregiver to growing children and aging parents—none of those experiences took place in a way, or in a part of the world, that made sense with how he was raised. Political and economic circumstances in his life forced him to grow up quickly. He had put his body on the line every day with the work he did on the ships. Who was looking out for his mental health? Nobody in the family ever asked Dad what he did to keep food on the table—it was just expected that he go out and do it, to be a silent provider. Dad had once told me that he didn't share with his siblings the details of the work he did as a sailor until they all went back to Nawan Pind in 2014 to scatter their parents' ashes. Dad said he hadn't told them the story before because nobody ever asked him about it—not his parents or his siblings.

As a Punjabi man, Dad wasn't raised in a society that valued or made space for men to talk about their emotions. It was more common for men of his generation to drink away their feelings and bottle up the pains they felt inside. I went to school with Punjabi friends who had alcoholic fathers. I had lost uncles who drank themselves to death. I'm grateful that Dad wasn't one of them. I'm grateful that, in a material sense, I was always cared for when it came to food, clothing, and shelter. Emotionally though, I felt like Dad's love was dependent upon how I lived up to the expectations he had of me. Because of the way our relationship was built, I didn't feel like I could ever talk to him about my fears, insecurities, or any factors that were making it harder for me to achieve and accomplish to his standards; I imagined that he would perceive it as an excuse. As a person who embodied hard work and didn't ever make excuses for himself, I didn't think Dad would understand where I was coming from. However, in that moment when I came forward and told him about my depression, he listened. Despite his initial resistance, he didn't brush me off. All those years I spent in my depression, I just wanted someone to see me, but in that moment, it felt like Dad and I finally saw each other.

COLLAPSE
C
17

In 1897, writer and activist WEB DuBois coined the term 'double consciousness' to describe what it was like to be Black in America. DuBois explained that being Black while navigating through an environment that systemically oppresses Black people came with the extra weight of "always looking at one's self through the eyes of others, of measuring one's soul by the tape of a world that looks on in amused contempt and pity." It is the persistent phenomenon of experiencing the world and viewing the self through one's own perspective, while also looking at the self through the harsh lens of an oppressive and judgmental society. Double consciousness can exist at an interpersonal level through our everyday interactions with other people, and at an institutional level in our dealings with employers, teachers, doctors, and law enforcement.

Like most matters of race and social justice, I first learned of the concept of double consciousness through a rap song. When I was in ninth grade, Toronto rap legend Kardinal Offishall released a song titled "Man by Choice." In the song, he says to the listener "it don't matter what you call yourself—it's what they call you behind your back." He then opens his verse by describing the ways in which racism and double consciousness have affected how he carries himself through the world, stating "I was born a regular man of the earth/ with a curse to walk like a soldier since birth/ my exterior is shaded in by my melanin/ stereotype of my type is a felon."

Through colonization and migration, the concept of double consciousness has been adapted by many different diasporic cultures that have lived through their own unique challenges as minorities and racialized peoples in the West. As a Sikh with a turban and beard, the place where my experience with double consciousness is most pronounced is at airports. In my travels, I am constantly reminded of my otherness, and the world around me has told me time and time again that it is fearful of me and views me with suspicion.

The not-so-random random selections for additional security screening is something I've come to expect at airports worldwide. There are the odd instances when I'll pass through without the extra hassle, but for the majority of the time, I know what to expect: additional luggage searches, body and head pat-downs, testing for explosive residue, and being sequestered in private rooms for one-on-one questioning to figure out where I'm going and why. I had let go of the hope that these checks were in any way random when I once travelled with a group of twelve relatives. As the only one in the group with a dastaar and beard, I was singled out by airport security and had my luggage opened and examined on the floor of the airport after landing. Even Sikhs who had achieved mainstream success and fame—like actor and designer Waris Ahluwalia—weren't spared from being singled out. The message I've internalized is that I'm seen as the potential terror with a propensity for violence; the onus is never on others to change, but on me to figure out how to present myself as less threatening.

I experience double consciousness in every step of the travelling process. When I board a plane and call my parents to let them know that I'm safe and preparing for takeoff, I can feel the other passengers staring daggers through me as I speak Punjabi. I imagine that they're wondering who I'm talking to and whether I'm communicating a plot so sinister that it can't be spoken aloud in English. I make sure to stay close to my bags at all times to avoid having someone think that I've abandoned a suitcase full of explosives. I try to travel light; I cram as much as I can into my backpack and carry-on luggage to avoid having to check any bags in. The less time I have to spend going through security, the better off I feel I'll be.

I tried to prepare Nuvi for all of this when we travelled together for the first time in November 2015 for her cousin's wedding in California. Our trip was scheduled to start in the Bay Area. After the wedding, we would fly from San Francisco to San Diego for a few days, drive up to Los Angeles to do some sightseeing, and then return to San Diego before flying back home. The itinerary involved three flights in ten days. I prefaced Nuvi by telling her that we had to be at the airport extra early to account for the delays that always seemed to pop up whenever I travelled by plane.

The flights from Toronto to San Francisco, and from San Francisco to San Diego came with the additional security screenings—as I had anticipated—but it was nothing out of the ordinary. It didn't ever feel good to be treated that way, but the random screenings didn't delay us for too long. Besides, it was hard to hold on to that bitterness when surrounded by the beauty of California—the mountains, the sunshine, the farms, the ocean. As a lifelong fan of *The Simpsons*, I had a blast being transported to Springfield at the Universal Studios theme park, and as a hip hop head, there was nothing better than seeing Kendrick Lamar perform the entirety of his *To Pimp a Butterfly* album in LA with a live band. Before the flight from San Diego to Toronto, I even made it through the security check without being randomly selected—or so I thought.

When I pulled my carry-on luggage from the conveyor and set it on the ground, a security guard ran over with his arms outstretched to block my passage.

"Help! I need some assistance here!" he shouted. He kept his head down and his eyes on the floor in front of him.

"Is there something wrong?" I asked him. Nuvi had already passed through the security check and was on the other side of the man who refused to let me through. I made eye contact with her. She looked worried.

"I said I need some help here," the man called again. Other passengers gathered around to watch after being alerted by the guard's hollering.

The man didn't respond to my question. "Can I go?" I asked again.

"There's an extra step," he replied. He kept his focus on the floor.

After now being stopped on each of my last three flights, I was growing frustrated. If this man wasn't going to at least look me in the eye and use some professional courtesy, I didn't see any reason to extend the same decency to him.

"For what?" I felt like I spat the words out of my mouth. Historically, I've tried not to show my irritation with people in authority, whether with teachers, the police, or at the airport. No matter how many times I get stopped and called in for more questioning, I try to speak calmly and in a respectful manner in our interactions; anger would only confirm the suspicions and stereotypes already held of me. At this point though, I didn't care. Maybe it wasn't the best way for me to handle the situation, but I was aggravated. I looked over at Nuvi again. Her worried expression had grown into fear.

"Amrit, just leave it," Nuvi pleaded. "Please. I just want us to get home."

"This guy can't even look at me and treat me like a human being," I shot back. I could feel my heartbeat pounding in my ears.

"It's your headgear," the man said. His arms were still held out at his sides, his eyes still downward.

"What about it?" I asked. A part of me was glad to hear him say that, to hear someone finally confirm my frustrations that this was a form of profiling and not random in any way.

"There's an extra step," he said again.

The fact that he couldn't explain himself allowed me to loosen the tension I held in my shoulders. This was an issue of laws and policies far bigger than this one person being paid to enforce them; this man was just a cog in the system. A colleague came in and relieved the man. The onlookers dispersed.

When I completed the additional screening and got to my gate, Nuvi asked me if I was okay. I told her I wasn't. There's always an extra step, I said. On the flight home, I tried to let the moment go, but my mind wouldn't rest. I thought about the way fear can be fueled by misinformation. I reflected on how prejudice can become policy, and how the fears held by the few can reign over the dignity of the many to become as restrictive, unbending, and systemic as law.

I put my headphones on and looked out the plane's window at the clouds drifting by. Music had always been a portal that allowed me to see beyond myself; it opened me up to the experiences and emotions of others, and helped me find connection and strength. I played Kendrick Lamar's *To Pimp a Butterfly* album and felt empowered. He reminded me that hate can't hold us back, and even though institutionalized oppression evolves and takes different forms, through our continued resilience, we would be all right.

***

Mom completed her schedule of radiation and chemo just before Christmas 2017.

January of the new year felt like a fresh start. Mom was turning a corner in her recovery and getting back to her old self. She had started going to physiotherapy to exercise and rebuild her thinning muscles. At home, she began her mornings by walking laps around the main floor of the house, looping between the dining room and kitchen for ten minutes at a time and swinging her arms at her sides with each step. Before she got sick, Mom used to go for walks in the ravine behind our house. She enjoyed being close to the streams, trees, and small lakes that lined the pathway. Sometimes she took roti and bread crumbs with her to feed the ducks. Her walks inside the house weren't as lengthy as the hour-long treks she used to do on the trail, but she was getting some of her endurance back.

Dad had returned to his normal schedule, no longer flexing his hours or missing days at work to accommodate Mom's appointments. I had completed my internship at the mental health agency and was working there full-time while still doing work with youth in the arts on the side. Nuvi was still tied up in the political world. None of us were around the house much during the daytime, so Mom was spending more time alone. She could fend for herself now though. She bathed herself and made her own tea. She was on a liquid diet, but she made her own fruit smoothies and oatmeal. We were still waiting on Mom's appointment with Dr. Higgins in April to hear whether she would need more chemo or radiation, but the family felt that Mom was getting stronger.

I sat at the dinner table with my parents on a cheerful and bright Sunday afternoon in mid-January. Since Mom's diagnosis and surgery, I hadn't spoken to her about her past the same way I had been doing with Dad—the here and now was difficult enough for her, I reasoned—but since Mom was progressing in her recovery, I wanted to take the time to learn about her life as well, and hear her reflect on where she'd been.

"After the fire on the ship, I was back in Nawan Pind for almost two years," Dad said. The fire in Bahrain had forced him and Raj to return to Punjab in the spring of 1978, less than a year after they left home for Europe. Dad was wearing a black Adidas tracksuit with gold stripes down the sleeves. On all the other days of the week, he only changed out of his work clothes and into his kurtha when he was ready to pray and go to bed. On Sundays, when he wasn't working on a project around the house, he liked to dress down. "I was getting older," he said. "I was almost twenty-five years old. My parents wanted me to get married."

"Who paired you and Mom together?" I asked. Arranged marriages were the common way most Punjabi weddings from my parents' generation took place.

"My grandparents made the match. I didn't have much of a say in it," Dad explained. He made the process seem very transactional, like it was just something that had to be done. "Parents had all the control back then. I knew I would have to get married eventually, so they arranged everything and I just had to agree with it."

Mom nodded. She had on an orange shawl, with one end of it thrown over her left shoulder to cover her radiation burns.

"You weren't nervous at all?" I asked.

"I knew your Mom's parents and had respect for them," Dad said. "She respected my parents too. What was there to be nervous about?"

"The timing was a bit rushed with the way it came together," Mom detailed. "I was getting ready to go to Canada when our wedding plans were being made."

Mom explained that Kulwinder Massi Ji had obtained Canadian citizenship in the mid-seventies and was in the process of sponsoring Mom, Amarjit Mamma Ji, Nani Ji, and Nana Ji to join her in Mississauga. My parents' wedding date hadn't been set yet, but a plan was in place for them to be married soon.

"Sponsorship wasn't easy to come by," Mom said. "We knew a lot of people around our village with family in Canada or the UK who had their sponsorship applications rejected. We might not have been fully aware of what we were getting into or where we were going, but when an opportunity for sponsorship came up, we had to take it. March 28, 1980—that's when I arrived in Canada. When I think about how long we've lived here, and then how long we were in Punjab before that, it almost feels like I've lived two lives."

Upon landing in Canada, Mom lived with Bachittar Massar Ji and Kulwinder Massi Ji in their two-floor, three-bedroom home in Mississauga. Mom and Nani Ji slept in one room, Massar Ji and Massi Ji slept in another room with their two children, Massar Ji's brother Harbhajan and his pregnant wife Sukhminder slept in the other bedroom with their son, and Amarjit Mamma Ji and Nana Ji slept in the basement.

I was familiar with the concept of the nest—the idea that the person most established would open their home to other relatives who were new to the country. Once they had jobs and had saved enough money and developed their own wings, the baby birds would leave the nest; however, they could always return if they fell and needed the support again. My parents eventually left Massar Ji and Massi Ji's nest in the mid-eighties to create one of their own. For most of my life, we've had different family members living with us at different times. During my childhood, we supported Kuldip Bhua Ji, Dhadha Ji, and Dhadhi Ji, and later Sardara Chacha Ji and Sukhi Chachi Ji, when they were new to the country. Even after my parents, Vijay, and I moved into our own home in Brampton in 1998, we still opened our doors to other relatives who needed a place to stay. When I was in middle school, Dad's cousin and her two sons were fleeing an abusive home. Dad took them in for a year and a half until they were able to move out on their own. When I was in university, my cousin Raman from Punjab stayed with us when she first came to Canada as an international student. Our homes were never silos; we were meant to flourish together.

"When I came to Canada, all the kids in the house were under five years old at that time," Mom explained. "Your Nani got pneumonia as soon as we landed. I was the only one who wasn't working then so I had to take care of everyone. All of that labour fell on me and it was hard." Mom noted that Massi Ji worked at a furniture manufacturing factory called Standard Upholstery back then, and she had helped Mom get a job there. "I was paid $3.50 an hour to do piecework. It was the first job I ever had," Mom smiled. As much as labour jobs seemed to break Mom's body down, she felt proud to be able to work; it made her feel like she had a purpose.

"It was a hard adjustment," she expanded. "One thing I remember— and it was a simple thing, but it was the hardest thing for me to get used to when I started working in Canada—was that in Punjab, whether we were cooking or cleaning or sewing, we mostly worked while sitting down or squatting. In Canada, we were always standing. We weren't allowed to rest unless someone else told us it was okay to do so. I remember how much my legs hurt and how heavy my boots felt at the end of every shift."

"When your mom was getting ready to go to Canada, I was still in Punjab," Dad added. "The plan was for her to sponsor me once she got settled out there. I felt I only had a few years left to make money for my parents before I left the village and joined your mom. I wanted to leave them with something more before I went to Canada myself, so I planned to go work in Europe again."

"You and Raj went back out for a third time?" I asked. After how badly their last excursion had ended, I didn't think they would go through with it again.

"There was nothing else to do in the village," Dad explained. "I was just waiting until the wedding. We still needed the money. This time, it was me and Raj and my friend Boota that travelled together. Boota's uncle asked me to take him to Europe with us."

As the person who had first put Dad in touch with The Coyote in the early seventies, Boota and his uncle felt Dad owed them this favor in return. Dad had known Boota since elementary school and their stories were similar: Boota was from a farming family, and had a debt of tens of thousands of rupees owed to private lenders. Another victim of The Green Revolution. The more Boota learned about the success Dad had working in Europe, the more he wanted to do the same to provide for his own family. Boota had heard about how things went sideways in Bachittar Massar Ji's and Dad's dealings with travel agents; Boota trusted that by travelling with Dad, he wouldn't be taken advantage of.

"Weren't you worried about that—being responsible for leading another person to Europe?" I asked Dad. I thought about the challenges I faced in my travels when just vacationing to different countries. I couldn't imagine the tension Dad must have felt when travelling without the proper documents and trying to find work, all while trying not to get caught.

"Boota's uncle was an elder," Dad explained, "so we didn't question him."

Part of the past fractures in my relationship with Dad stemmed from expectation. When I was younger and he asked me to do something, he needed it done right away and to the best of my capabilities. He didn't permit space for backtalk. Schools and pop culture in the West told me I had autonomy and choice, even as a kid. The way Dad was brought up in Punjab though, he had to do as he was told, even as an adult. If he was told to get married, he did it without asking questions. If he was told to take someone to Europe despite the risks that came with it, he did it. It was the same for Mom when she first came to Canada as well, having to be the caretaker for the kids and for the sick in a home with so many people in it.

In the late seventies and early eighties, Mom and Dad felt like their lives were being laid out for them, and they had to fall in line and follow orders. However, in Dad's third trip to Europe, he discovered that even the best laid plans can fall apart.

***

Satnam, Raj, and Boota each set aside close to 20 000 rupees for their journey to Greece. Their goal was to find work in the ship yards in Piraeus, and they decided that taking the same route out of Punjab again, starting in Nepal, would be the best way there. Satnam and Raj paid for their flights out of pocket, and Boota got his funds through private lenders.

Before leaving Punjab, Satnam's previous passport had run out of pages. He had to get a new passport made from the office in Chandigarh, which was granted on May 26, 1979. The officials at the passport office sewed Satnam's new passport to his old one with a red thread, indicating that the two documents were continuations of each other, and that they needed to be displayed and reviewed in tandem any time he travelled. A wax seal was placed on top of the thread to prevent any tampering or separation of the passports.

Before the trio flew from Punjab to Kathmandu in May 1980, Satnam hid himself in the washroom stalls at the airport in Amritsar. He used a pocketknife to remove the wax stamp and pluck apart the thread that held his old and new passports together, freeing the fresh passport for use without any records or evidence of the countries he had previously been to in his travels over the last several years. He wrapped his old passport in clothes and buried it at the bottom of his suitcase like a skeleton kept in a shallow grave.

After arriving in Nepal, Satnam, Raj, and Boota flew from Kathmandu to Bangkok on tourist visas and arrived in Thailand on May 21, 1980. While in Bangkok, they obtained tourist visas for Poland on May 26. Before they could leave Bangkok though, Satnam developed an intense fever. Diarrhea and migraines soon followed. Satnam tried to soldier on, but Raj didn't see how he would be able to travel the rest of the way in this condition. Despite Satnam's protests, Raj took him to a hospital to get checked out. Satnam was diagnosed with typhoid fever and had to dip into their limited reservoir of money to cover medical costs. Boota suggested that he and Raj go to Greece together, leaving Satnam in the hospital or sending him back home to Punjab if he wasn't well enough to travel any further. Raj refused to leave Satnam's side. Understanding that their finances were being eaten away the longer he stayed in hospital, Satnam discharged himself after five days. They flew from Bangkok to Poland on June 6, 1980.

***

"Sir, I can't let you through."

Satnam, Raj, and Boota were in Malmö, Sweden. It was June 1980. Satnam was twenty-six years old. After they had arrived in Poland, they flew to Sweden for what was supposed to be their last stop on the way to Greece. A Swedish customs official with icy blue eyes and golden blonde hair stood behind a glass panel at Sturup Airport in Malmö and stopped them for questioning.

"There are only 800 American dollars here between the three of you," the agent said. He slid the envelope of money back to Satnam through an opening at the bottom of the glass panel that separated them. After the unexpected stay at the hospital in Bangkok, there wasn't much money left. "We've had issues of migrant workers here lately. People travelling without sufficient documentation. Surely you understand my concerns over how three men can book hotel rooms, buy food, and do all the things that tourists do with such a small budget. That is, if you are tourists."

Satnam was afraid this might happen. To embellish the amount of money he, Raj, and Boota still had left, Satnam had bundled their remaining cash so that the bills of larger denomination were on the outside of the pile. The rest of the stack consisted of one-dollar bills to make the wad look thicker. The agent paused, cold eyes drilling through the glass. He waited for an explanation.

Satnam pulled out another envelope from the chest pocket of his jacket. He laid it on the table and handed it to the agent. "We're not planning to stay in Sweden for very long," Satnam noted. "From here, we're going to England and then flying right back to India."

The agent opened the envelope. Inside of it were three plane tickets scheduled to depart in a few weeks from Heathrow Airport in London for the destination of Delhi. The agent examined the tickets. Raj and Boota looked to each other out of the corners of their eyes. Neither of them said a word.

"After a few days here in Sweden, I'll be taking my friends to stay with my cousin over in England," Satnam explained to the agent. "He has a house in Derby, so we don't have to worry about hotels. He'll feed us too. If you're a guest in a Punjabi home, you don't ever have to pay for anything," Satnam chuckled. Raj and Boota followed suit and laughed with him. "$800 is enough for us until we get to England. Believe me."

The agent put the tickets in the envelope and handed them back to Satnam. "Sorry for the delay," the agent said.

Neither Satnam, Raj, nor Boota spoke until they were outside the airport. Cabs and limos pulled up to the curb in front of them and waited for other passengers. The three friends stood behind a concrete pillar to stay out of sight.

"England? What's going on?" Boota asked. "What happened to Greece?"

"We're not going to England," Satnam responded. He looked over his shoulder to make sure no one was listening in. "I asked my cousin Gurmukh in England to buy these plane tickets for us in case something like this happened—to protect us. He mailed them to me just before the three of us left home for Nepal."

"The agents are on to us," Boota said. "I told you we shouldn't have stopped in that hospital in Bangkok. If we still had all that cash we wasted there, no one would be suspicious of us now."

"If we left Satnam in the hospital like you wanted, we wouldn't have had those plane tickets to save us just now," Raj fired back.

"Okay, stop, that's enough" Satnam interjected. "Keep your voices down. If they think $800 isn't enough for three people, we shouldn't travel together then, right? What if we split the money three ways and just go straight to Crete from here? We find the earliest flights out and each of us travels on our own. We can meet at the same hotel that Raj and I stayed at last time. Once we're all there, we'll go to Piraeus together and find work."

Boota offered to fly first. He didn't want to stay in Sweden any longer than necessary after the close call with the customs official. Satnam divided the money equally among the three of them. They found a hotel room to stay for the night with the intention of looking for flights to Crete first thing in the morning.

***

Before Boota left Sweden for Greece, Satnam gave him the address of the designated hotel where they would all meet. Satnam obtained a tourist visa from the Greek embassy in Sweden on June 25, 1980 and flew out a day after Boota did. Raj arrived in Greece several hours after Satnam. When the two of them got to the hotel in Crete, Boota wasn't there. They searched the surrounding neighbourhoods and popular tourist spots, but Boota was nowhere to be found.

"We've got to go," Raj said to Satnam. They were in their hotel room together. All the lights in the room were off. They hadn't unpacked or slept since arriving in Crete nearly two days ago. "We can't stay here and just look for Boota forever. Our visas are going to expire. I say we go to Piraeus and get jobs for ourselves. With any luck, for all we know, maybe Boota already made his way to the shipyard on his own and found work for himself."

Satnam wasn't lifted by Raj's optimism this time. Satnam shook his head and looked through the room's parted curtains towards the beach. The sands were just as white as he remembered, the waters still just as turquoise and clear.

"He wouldn't go without us," Satnam said. "He was so scared—about leaving Punjab, about getting caught. He wouldn't do something like that on his own."

"We can't stay here," Raj urged.

Satnam thought about filing a missing person's report. He couldn't turn to the police for help without exposing his own immigration status and incriminating himself though. He looked back towards Raj who stood just inside the doorway of the room.

"You said we wouldn't be running like this for the rest of our lives," Satnam said. "Now it feels like we're never going to stop." He took a last look out at the beach and closed the curtains. He followed Raj out the door and the two left Crete for Piraeus.

***

In Piraeus, Satnam and Raj scoured the ports for Boota. They asked the other South Asian workers they met in the shipyards if they had spoken to anyone who matched Boota's name or description, but nobody had seen him. It was like he had vanished. Satnam and Raj went to the same employment agency they had visited twice before and got jobs together working with Captain Alex once again. They were flown to Spain the next day for their first delivery.

News of Boota's whereabouts wouldn't arrive until several months later. Upon docking in Morocco to deliver cargo, Satnam received a letter from his parents. They explained that Boota did arrive in Crete and he did check himself into the hotel as instructed, but he grew impatient with waiting for Raj and Satnam to join him. Boota was approached by a couple of South Asian migrant workers in Crete, and they asked if Boota was interested in working with them on a farm. Boota checked out of the hotel before Satnam and Raj could arrive from Sweden, and took a job where he was paid in cash under the table by a Greek farm owner.

The letter said that Boota and the men who had invited him to work on the farm were apprehended by Greek immigration officials after five months, and they were subsequently deported back to India. Satnam felt like this was all his fault. He had been tasked with keeping Boota safe and guiding him to jobs and opportunity. It was his plan that left Boota in Crete alone. Satnam felt like he had abandoned his friend.

***

One morning in January 2018, I received a phone call at work from my sister Vijay. She said she was in her car and following an ambulance to the hospital. Mom had an accident.

Vijay explained that earlier that day, Mom went down to the cold storage room in the basement to grab a handful of apples to place in a fruit basket in the dining room upstairs. She cradled five or six apples in her arms and held them close to her chest. When Mom got to the top of the stairs, one of the apples fell loose and tumbled a few steps down. When she turned to see where it had landed, she got dizzy and her blood pressure dropped. Mom fell down the stairs head first. Her face slammed into each step on the way down.

Vijay told me that she had been getting ready for work in the basement bathroom when she heard Mom fall. She opened the bathroom door when she heard the thuds, and found Mom on the floor at the bottom of the steps. Mom tried to get to her feet but she couldn't raise herself higher than her hands and knees. Blood poured out of her head from multiple cuts. Vijay told Mom to stop struggling and to lay down. She put a towel to Mom's head to stop the bleeding but the gashes in her forehead were so deep that they exposed bone. Mom was upset that Vijay had called an ambulance; she said she didn't need their help and didn't want to go to the hospital.

In the ER, Mom had no idea where she was or what had happened. The trauma to her head had shaken the memory of the fall from her mind. X-rays confirmed that she had a concussion and a vertebrae fracture in her neck. When Mom came home from the hospital eight hours later, her face was bruised purple and her eyes were swollen shut. Her forehead was lined with a zipper of stitches and her neck was in a brace. I felt like all of Mom's progress had been derailed. Cancer stood across the blood-stained canvas on the other side of the ring from Mom, cackling and flaunting the life it had stolen from her like it was a trophy.

The doctors estimated Mom would need to keep the brace on for six weeks for the fracture to heal. It would come off at the end of March, just before she was scheduled to meet with Dr. Higgins in April. Until then, she had new appointments with the physiotherapist and the fracture clinic.

Mom was quiet for several days after her fall. She seemed upset at herself for falling, for setting back the progress of her recovery, and for not being strong enough yet. Mom started preparing for a future that she didn't see herself being part of, using statements like "if I'm not here next year," or "I don't know how much longer I have." She was losing her faith in any positive news coming in April. We were worried that Mom had given up on herself.

174

CHAPTER
EIGHTEEN

HOME

By February 2018, Mom still wore a dressing on the left side of her neck in the area where the radiation treatment had been localized. Changing the dressing became a two-person job ever since her fall down the stairs. Mom would lay on her back as I stabilized her head, while Dad unlatched and removed her neck brace to clean the skin and apply a new dressing. I was scared of touching Mom after her fall; with the vertebrae fracture, any slight movement would send lightning rods of pain shooting through her body. I didn't want to cause her any more agony.

One evening after changing Mom's dressing, Dad and I sat on the floor in her room. Mom sat on her bed with a blanket over her legs. She watched an Indian singing competition on TV, but she wasn't smiling. Since her fall, it became more difficult for her to speak as her neck brace pushed her chin up and compressed her face. It was dark out but Mom preferred to keep the lights in the room off.

"It was a hard job," Dad shared, trying to summarize his years working on cargo ships.

He explained that his third tour of the seas had taken him to new destinations like China, Sri Lanka, and Japan for the first time. From Osaka, his ship took a load of cars and pickup trucks to Myanmar. Before departing Myanmar, Dad's freighter filled up on a rice shipment to take to Cuba, a trip that would take forty days to complete and was his longest single delivery.

"It was a dangerous job too—to be on the oceans for years like that and not know how to swim," Dad explained. "A lot of my success and safety came down to luck. I didn't always know what I was doing, but I still took chances and they mostly paid off."

"Did you ever see Boota again?" I asked.

Dad straightened his back. He constricted his lips and turned his mouth into a frown. He shook his head slightly.

Dad detailed the series of events that led to him and Boota eventually meeting again. From Cuba, Dad sailed to New Orleans to load up on a cargo of cattle feed. Upon entering the US, he called Bachittar Massar Ji to let him know that he had arrived safely. Massar Ji explained that the sponsorship application that Mom had filed for Dad to join them in Canada was being reviewed. Massar Ji advised Dad to go back to India as soon as possible to prepare for the interview, which was the last step of the sponsorship process.

The next morning, Dad told Captain Alex that he was quitting the crew for good to be with his family. Alex informed Dad that he was in line for a promotion. The shipping company had purchased a new Japanese cargo ship and they needed a crew of thirty people to help run it. Alex felt Dad had all the qualities to make a great captain and hoped that he would be willing to go back to Punjab to gather a crew of men with work ethics just like his to help run the ship. Alex didn't know what Dad had to do to keep coming back to Europe time after time; Dad never told him either.

"I just laughed to myself," Dad said. "I thought about how I would get thirty men from Punjab to Greece without the proper visas when I couldn't even get Boota out safely. I turned the offer down and thanked the captain for the opportunity. When I got back to Punjab, Boota and his uncle both wanted to see me. Boota felt that I took advantage of him, that I stole his money." Dad turned his head away from me and faced the TV, though it didn't seem like he was paying attention to what he was looking at. "I didn't hide anything from Boota at any point during that trip—he and Raj both knew where every dollar went," Dad noted. "I apologized to Boota for splitting us up in Sweden. It wasn't the best move, but we were scared. We didn't want to get caught."

"Did you say all that to him?" I asked. It didn't seem like Dad wanted to go into much detail. I felt like I was picking at an old scab of his that hadn't fully healed yet, and my questions were breaking the skin open once more.

"He didn't want to listen," Dad explained. "I stopped talking after a while and just let Boota yell and say everything he needed to get off his mind. I didn't see him again for years after that."

After he had failed to clear the air with Boota, Dad went to Delhi and had his sponsorship interview. After a twenty-minute conversation, Dad was approved for entry into Canada.

Suddenly, Mom let out a gasp. Dad and I both turned towards her. She leaned forward with her head down and her hand on the back of her brace. Her fingers tried to claw through the grey plastic so she could soothe her skin. Dad climbed on to the bed next to her.

"What's wrong?" he asked. He placed a hand on her shoulder.

Mom tried to say something but the brace blocked her jaw from moving. Mom swiped a hand at us, demanding that we back off and give her space. She mumbled something again, but we couldn't make out what it was. Dad asked her to repeat herself.

"Pain," she said. She lifted her head. The light from the television exposed glimmering tears in her eyes. "Too much pain."

***

Before Mom got sick, Dad was planning to retire on his 65th birthday in October 2018. With Mom's condition worsening after her fall though, the family didn't want to leave her home alone and risk another accident. Dad couldn't keep up with his regular job while also taking Mom to her growing list of appointments with the physiotherapist, fracture clinic, family doctor, pain management clinic, and follow-up appointments with the radiation specialist. By February 2018, Dad decided to retire to take care of Mom. In 1975, family was the reason why Dad left home for the world. Now, family would be the reason why he left the world behind and stayed home.

CHAPTER 19

As a kid growing up in the early nineties, my family made multiple trips to the gurudwara in Malton every week. The langar hall in the basement of the gurudwara was a place where the community gathered to prepare, serve, and eat food together. Over the sound of clattering metal dishes, people sat on rows of black mats rolled out on the tiled floor and discussed Gurbani, family life, and politics in Canada and Punjab while they sipped cha and ate their meals.

The langar halls of my youth were lined with framed pictures of young Sikh women and men clutching AK-47s and revolvers as closely as kin. These images were hung next to photos of garland-adorned bodies laid out with severed limbs and bloodstained clothes. As a kid, I had no context as to how long ago this all happened, who these people were, what causes they fought and died for, and what forced them to abandon the youth that I reveled in. There was no explanation for the graphic nature of the images but I couldn't escape how commonplace these pictures were, showing up not only in the gurudwaras we attended, but also in various widely-circulated Punjabi newspapers that I saw tucked under the arms of elderly men at bus stops. My parents, aunties, uncles, and grandparents knew the stories behind each of those pictures and they talked about it amongst themselves, but never in front of us kids. It created a confusing environment as a child where I was aware that people who looked like my parents were being killed but I didn't know why, when, or where.

Clarity wouldn't come until I got to university. Through activities and student clubs on campus, I met new people and made new friends, many of whom were also Sikh. In getting to know them, we talked about our upbringings. Some of them shared their experiences of growing up in places like Winnipeg and Guelph, towns that were mostly white and much different from the multicultural neighbourhoods like Malton and Brampton where I was raised. Some of our conversations focused on Sikhi, whether we grew up feeling connected to it, and how often we visited gurudwaras with our families. One thing I learned was that regardless of where we were from, the images in the langar halls were the same for all of us. After speaking with my friends, I wanted to learn more about the background behind those photographs to try and understand what it was that our community was documenting and why.

I began my research online and learned about the violence that Sikh civilians suffered at the hands of the Indian government, police, and military in the eighties and nineties. I read about how mobs armed with iron rods and kerosene descended upon Sikh villages and businesses; how Sikh women were gang-raped; how bodies were set aflame with tires around their necks; how chemical weapons like white phosphorous were used against Sikhs; how burnt bodies were stacked on top of each other in despairing piles; and how historical Sikh libraries were burned to the ground. What made it hurt more was that this was still recent history, close enough in time that many of the slain and the survivors were people from my parents' generation. Most of my friends were also coming across this information for the first time as they too grew up with families like mine who kept a shroud of silence around why lives were being taken.

The more research I did into this period of time, the more I found that older generations differed in how they viewed that era of India's history. Mom was upset that I was digging up old bones. "You can't do anything to save those people now," she said. "Let the dead rest." My friends and I started organizing events to talk about these traumas through arts-based expression, and panels with human rights activists and survivors of police torture. However, some of my relatives didn't want me to participate in these events. From their perspective, simply engaging with our history was too political of an act. We were in Canada now, they reasoned; we were safe here, and I shouldn't do anything that could potentially jeopardize how my future employers would view me. Go to school, get a job; become part of the system, don't disturb it. I argued what good was a system that promoted multiculturalism but didn't allow space for people from different cultures to discuss the politics and traumas that led to them having to leave home in the first place? My friends and I decided that it was more important to create that space for ourselves than it was to enjoy the comfort and privilege afforded by our status as model minorities in Canada.

Dad responded opposite to the way Mom did, and he brought books home for me that provided even more context to the pictures I saw in the langar halls. I learned that the events that took place in India in the eighties were not new fights. In my readings, I discovered that prior to partition, the state of Punjab in northern India was home to Muslims, Hindus, and Sikhs. While Muslims were a minority in India, making up a quarter of the country's population, they constituted a majority within Punjab. In 1940, while India was still a British colony, a movement calling for an independent Muslim nation to be carved out of India grew in popularity. Led by Muhammad Ali Jinnah, this push to separate from India and to create the new nation of Pakistan was intended to protect the rights of the Muslim minority. Though Sikhs were also a minority in India who made up only two percent of the national population, they considered Punjab to be their historical homeland as the Sikh religion was founded there, Punjab was home to eighty percent of all Indian Sikhs, and Punjab was the heart of the Sikh kingdom that had been in place for fifty years before the British colonized the region.

As India approached partition and independence, Indian Prime Minister Jawaharlal Nehru sought to develop a constitution based around autonomy for states. To assure Sikhs that their language, culture, and way of life would not be lost, Nehru stated that "the brave Sikhs of Punjab are entitled to special considerations. I see nothing wrong in an area set up in the north of India wherein the Sikhs can also experience the glow of freedom."

After two centuries of colonial rule, the last viceroy of British India, Louis Mountbatten, was tasked with facilitating England's exit from the Indian subcontinent. Mountbatten gave barrister Cyril Radcliffe—who had never set foot in India before—the difficult job of drawing the new borders that were to satisfy Indian and Pakistani sentiments. To make matters even more challenging, Mountbatten gave Radcliffe just five weeks to complete the task. In a botched and rushed job, the new borders drawn up by Radcliffe at partition ran right through the state of Punjab, allocating the majority of Punjab's land and resources to Pakistan, and leaving the remainder in India. This sparked mass migration and widespread violence throughout India and Pakistan. The exact death toll from the fallout of partition isn't known, but estimates place it in the hundreds of thousands. A chilling detail I had learned from Dhadha Ji's sister Chanan Kaur was that after partition, the wind carried the stench of dead bodies all the way to her village for days on end.

With the British now gone, when Nehru was asked about the considerations he had promised to make for Sikhs, he stated that "the circumstances have now changed." The federal Indian constitution granted more power to the central government than it did to individual states. Unhappy with these developments, the Sikh representative on the committee that helped draft India's constitution protested by refusing to sign it. Punjab's governor Chandu Lal Trivedi issued a statement that tried to drive a further wedge along religious lines, calling Sikhs lawless and expressing that special measures should be taken against them so they wouldn't disrupt law-abiding Hindus.

An independent India struggled to deal with what the British had left behind. Many of the existing state borders in India were relics that represented past British political and military strategy, but had no relevance to the cultures of the people who lived in those states. The Indian government decided that a reorganization of state borders on the basis of language was necessary to allow for easier communication, administration, and governance. Nehru's decision to change borders to accurately represent language was also influenced by the creation of the state of Andhra Pradesh in southern India in 1953, which was formed after Telugu-speaking people engaged in hunger strikes and protests to create their own linguistic state.

Seeing this as an opportunity for Sikhs to protect and preserve their mother tongue, the Akali Dal, a political party that represented Sikh interests, pushed for Punjabi to be recognized as the main language within Punjab. Dubbed the Punjabi Suba Movement, Sikhs regularly took to the streets to rally and shout slogans in support of their cause. This agitational campaign resulted in the Indian government imposing a ban on the use of these slogans. To spite the ban, over 10 000 Sikhs intentionally courted arrest by continuing to shout the slogans at rallies. Dad's uncle Mohan Singh was even arrested multiple times throughout the fifties and sixties for participating in protests that called for Punjab to become a Punjabi-speaking state. Harmandhir Sahib in Punjab had spiritually been an important gurudwara for Sikhs; it also gained political significance as Sikhs in the Punjabi Suba Movement gathered there to plan their next protests. On July 4, 1955, things turned violent. In a tactic designed to snuff out the movement, Punjab police launched tear gas at crowds inside the gurudwara complex and beat Sikhs with clubs and rifles.

In 1956, India's States Reorganization Commission went ahead with the plan to restructure many state borders on linguistic grounds. However, the Commission did not recognize Punjabi as being sufficiently distinct from Hindi. Of the fourteen official languages recognized in India's constitution, Punjabi was the only one after reorganization that did not have its own state. The identity of Sikhs was closely tied to the Punjabi language; the Akali Dal became more concerned that, as a minority, young Sikhs would lose their connection to their language and history due to the influence from larger religious and linguistic groups.

In 1966, Punjab's borders were restructured under the Punjab Reorganization Act. This left a Sikh, Punjabi-speaking majority within the state, while areas of Punjab with a Hindu majority were given the new state of Haryana. However, despite the delayed success of the Punjabi Suba Movement in finally creating a linguistic state, grievances between Sikhs and the Indian government were deepened when it came to matters of natural resources.

As Dad had shared with me, farming was a legacy that was passed down from generation to generation for centuries in many Sikh households, and the richness of Punjab's river waters had made that possible. Agriculture was the lifeblood of Punjab's economy and it accounted for over forty percent of the state's income. Under international law, and as outlined in India's constitution, if a river is contained entirely within the borders of one state, then that state alone would have control over how the river was used. Similarly, if a river flowed through multiple states, each state would have the right to make decisions on the portion of the river that passed through its borders. However, the constitution of the Punjab Reorganization Act gave the Indian government power to dictate how Punjab's river waters would be distributed. The Indian government made the decision to divert seventy-five percent of Punjab's water to other states like Haryana, Rajasthan, and Delhi. Conversely, the state of Punjab was not permitted to access waters in these other states. With the introduction of The Green Revolution and the demands it had placed on water resources, farmers had to exploit and deplete groundwater supplies to grow their HYV seeds. Farmers feared they wouldn't be able to sustain their farms under these conditions.

To express their discontent with how Sikhs had been treated along linguistic and socioeconomic grounds since partition, the Akali Dal created the Anandpur Sahib Resolution in 1973. The major aims of this document included allowing Sikhs to have autonomy over Punjab as was promised before partition, eliminating poverty through a more equitable distribution of wealth, the establishment of a minimum wage for the labour class, the removal of discrimination on the basis of caste or any other grounds, the recognition of Sikhi as a distinct and unique faith separate from Hinduism in the Indian Constitution, the removal of taxes on all agricultural lands and tractors so farmers could continue to earn a living, and granting Punjab autonomy over its water supply.

By putting the country in a state of emergency in June 1975, Indian Prime Minister Indira Gandhi had given herself more power than ever before. Members of the Akali Dal who had pushed forward the Anandpur Sahib Resolution were consequently jailed under Gandhi's rule. After decades of disenfranchisement, there was a rise in sentiment among Sikhs who felt that separating from India and forming an independent nation was the only way to preserve the Sikh identity and to have their voices heard. These tensions between Sikhs and the Indian government created a hostile climate that bubbled through the late seventies and early eighties, and boiled over in 1984.

The more I learned about Sikh struggles within India, the more I found Sikh people close to home within Brampton and Mississauga—colleagues, aunties, and uncles—who had personal experiences with state violence in India. They still carried with them the traumas they had suffered at the hands of the Indian government. My father also had a brush with state violence in the eighties, though he was fortunate enough to escape unscathed.

***

The post-wedding high still hadn't worn off. It was December 1981. Satnam was twenty-eight years old. He and Narinder were newly married on December 5 in a simple ceremony held in her family's village of Gillaan. A cook was hired to prepare food for all of the attendees who participated in the festivities. Guests filled up their plates with barfis and pakoray and spent their evenings dancing and singing songs. Narinder's brother Amarjit was married the following day—December 6—to his fiancée Sewa Kaur. Both siblings, Narinder and Amarjit, had immigrated to Canada in March 1980 and they only had a small window of time to visit Punjab and get married to their respective partners before they had to go back to their lives in Mississauga. To maximize what little time they had in the village, their parents had arranged for both weddings to take place on back-to-back days.

The celebrations in Gillan continued several days after the weddings had taken place. When the overnight guests sat down to drink cha and eat seerni in the mornings, their ears still rang with the echoes of laughter and handclaps from the long night of dancing the evening prior. In addition to the weddings, there were many other reasons to celebrate. Narinder's sponsorship application for Satnam to join her in Canada had been approved. Narinder's other brother Harjit, who had been living in the UK since the mid-seventies, travelled back to Punjab to see both of these weddings take place. It was the first time he had been back in Gillaan since he and his wife Nirmal had their first child together in England in May 1981. Life was expanding in size and scope, with partners and babies adding new limbs to the family tree that had now taken root in three continents. For Narinder, Harjit, and Amarjit, they weren't sure when they would have time like this again, to be together in the village where they all grew up; they wanted to savour every second of it that they could.

At the conclusion of a big family dinner in Gillaan a few days after the weddings, Satnam was prepared to finally take Narinder to his parents' house in Nawan Pind. By the time they had said their goodbyes and were ready to leave though, it was too late in the night and too dark out to commute by motorcycle along the unpaved country roads that connected the two villages. Satnam and Narinder decided to stay the night in Gillaan and leave in the morning when it was safer to travel.

The next morning before departure, Satnam decided to go for a walk around Gillaan to clear his head and take a break from the festivities.

"Mind if I join you?" Satnam's new brother-in-law Harjit asked. "Need to use the toilet." There was no bathroom in the family home in Gillaan; one had to travel to the facilities closer to the farm for relief.

"Sure," Satnam said. "I'm heading that way myself."

To protect against the early morning chill, Harjit and Satnam wrapped shawls around their shoulders. Harjit pulled his shawl over his mouth to keep his face warm. Seemingly appearing out of nowhere, a jeep screeched to a halt in front of them. Satnam coughed, choked by the clouds of dirt unsettled by the vehicle's tires. Two police officers emerged, identically clad in brown uniforms and caps.

"You two—show your faces," one of the officers shouted. They left their jeep doors open and the engine running. Both cops wore shiny silver shades that hid their eyes.

"Let's see some identification," the other officer demanded.

Harjit pulled his shawl down from his mouth and scoffed. "Don't need ID to go to the bathroom," he said. He and Satnam tried to continue their walk but the officers blocked their path.

"You," an officer pointed to Satnam. "What's your name?"

"Me?" Satnam asked. His legs went rigid and he froze.

"Yes, you. What is your name?"

"My name is Satnam."

"We're looking for someone in the area with that name," the other officer said. "A murder suspect. We need both of you to get on the ground now."

"What? I haven't killed anyone," Satnam argued. He tried to steady the tremble in his voice. "My in-laws live in this village and—"

Satnam stopped himself when he saw both officers grip the handles of their holstered batons. He and Harjit slowly lowered themselves to the ground and sat cross-legged in the street. From his seated position, Satnam could smell the leather from the cops' polished brown boots.

"Whatever you're saying he did, you're wrong," Harjit remarked to the officers. "He hasn't done anything like what you're accusing him of."

A few of Narinder's cousins heard the arguing and came out to talk to the officers. They explained that Satnam was bound for Canada in a few months and that Harjit was visiting from England. Narinder, her father, and a few other uncles and aunties who had spent the previous night there spilled out onto the road. Too big of a crowd for the cops to try anything, Satnam thought—too many witnesses. The officers radioed for back-up and a team of over twenty cops swarmed the village. They searched every room in Narinder's home, as well as several of her neighbours' houses. After two hours, the police said Satnam and Harjit were free to go.

"Are you okay?" Harjit asked while helping Satnam to his feet.

Satnam brushed the earth from the seat of his pants and didn't speak. He stared at the retreating police vehicles in the distance that vanished from sight just as suddenly as they had arrived. Satnam had heard stories of increased police violence in Punjab; he was aware of the way cops overstepped their authority and used intimidation and torture to get more information. Sometimes the cops beat people up just because they knew they wouldn't face any repercussions. Satnam was out of the country and working on the ships while most of these tensions unfolded though. The men he had met in West Germany, the ones who sought asylum to flee political persecution, had left Punjab for Europe because they were trying to escape this kind of treatment from the Indian state. Satnam didn't think he would ever experience the violence himself, especially this close to home.

***

The same way that pictures in langar halls told stories of a dark time in Sikh history, so too did the photographs in my family albums. However, our pictures told stories in ways that were less obvious than the ones we saw in the gurudwaras.

My sister Vijay was born in Toronto in June 1983 and looked to be about a year old in a picture that I had seen many times. In the photograph, she wore a pink, sleeveless onesie. Her mouth was open in laughter and her eyes were alight with joy. Nani Ji held Vijay with one arm and wore a white chunni wrapped around her sun-kissed face. They stood in the verandah of a house in Punjab that I didn't recognize, in front of a faded blue, wooden door that led to brown, concrete steps. Teal paint peeled off the wall behind them and exposed earth-toned bricks underneath.

As a child, a common picture I saw in the langar hall of every gurudwara I visited was that of a dilapidated Harmandhir Sahib. In the photo, the white exterior of the gurudwara complex was charred black by smoke and rocket fire. That was in June 1984 when the Indian government had killed hundreds of civilians inside the gurudwara as part of Operation Blue Star. Dad told me that the picture with Vijay and Nani Ji, for all of the peace and innocence that it represented, was taken just a few days before Operation Blue Star was launched.

Dad explained that he, Mom, and Vijay had visited Punjab in April 1984. It was the first time my parents had been back home in over two years, and it was the first time that Dhadha Ji and Dhadhi Ji—who still hadn't migrated to Canada by that point—met Vijay. Dad said that the energy in the air felt different in Punjab during that visit. He shared that the interactions between civilians and police in Punjab, like the one he had in Gillaan in 1981, had become more common by the spring of 1984. Police surveillance was heightened and the government cracked down on behaviors that they deemed suspicious: two people weren't permitted to ride on a single motorcycle together, it became illegal for four or more people to congregate in public spaces, and curfews were put in place to restrict movement after nightfall.

By May 1984, close to a month after my parents and sister had arrived in Punjab, Dad returned to Canada. This was shortly after my parents had just purchased their first home together. Dad had to get back to work to make sure the bills were paid. Mom decided to stay in Punjab for a little while longer. After experiencing her first few Canadian winters, she was homesick and missed the sun.

Political tensions in Punjab intensified in the weeks my parents spent apart. The Indian government instituted media blackouts in Punjab and placed a stranglehold on what information trickled in and out of the region. The more time my parents spent away from each other, the deeper Dad's regrets became about returning to Canada on his own. He felt like he had abandoned his wife and daughter in the middle of a political powder keg.

In Punjab, Mom tried to find a flight back to Canada but everything was sold out—there were too many other people trying to get out of Punjab at the same time due to the political instability. She eventually found two tickets on a flight that would bring her and Vijay home to Pearson International Airport in Toronto. Mom and Vijay travelled the eight-hour journey from Punjab to the airport in Delhi by bus and train with Nana Ji at their side. Police checkpoints stopped buses every few kilometres. Guards armed with rifles searched trains at every station. Mom sat with Vijay in her lap for the entire voyage and held her close so the gun barrels wouldn't brush up against her.

Nana Ji's job was only half done when he dropped Mom and Vijay off to the airport. He now had to make the entire trip back to Punjab from Delhi without a companion. His bus hurtled over the state line to re-enter Punjab just hours before the government locked down the borders. No one was allowed in or out for days after that. Mom and Vijay made it home to Dad in Canada on June 5, 1984. On June 6, Indira Gandhi gave the green light to commence Operation Blue Star, and the Indian military launched their attack on Harmandhir Sahib in Amritsar. Gandhi justified the move as being necessary to get rid of Sikh secessionists inside the gurudwara. However, reports indicate that anywhere from 1000 to 5000 innocent Sikh civilians were killed in the process.

Kuldip Bhua Ji was at school in Punjab when the attacks had occurred. Announcements over the loudspeakers ordered students to vacate campus property immediately. All schools stayed closed for weeks after that. In speaking with a colleague of mine at the mental health agency in Mississauga who had lived in Amritsar in 1984, he shared with me that the missiles fired by the Indian military during Operation Blue Star flew right over his home. The roar of the blast had knocked pictures off his walls. He could still remember how black smoke suffocated the sky, and how the smell of fire and death hung in the air.

In the aftermath of Operation Blue Star, Indira Gandhi was assassinated by her Sikh bodyguards on October 31, 1984. Anti-Sikh violence facilitated by Gandhi's Congress Party ravaged Delhi until November 3. The Congress Party used voter lists to identify Sikh homes and businesses, and distributed knives, iron rods, and flammable materials to death squads who were sent to kill Sikh civilians. Within my own family, Dhadhi Ji's brother-in-law was killed in Delhi in November 1984 while trying to stop a mob of people from attacking a village heavily populated by Sikhs. Human rights groups place the death toll of Sikhs in Delhi after Gandhi's assassination at 10 000.

***

My parents' connection to that time in history was a series of close calls. My wife Nuvi's family experienced that era in a more painful way as her Mamma Ji, Babla, was detained and tortured by Punjab police in 1986.

Following Operation Blue Star, the Indian government carried out Operation Woodrose. This gave police and military increased authority to capture Sikhs in the name of eradicating militancy. Thousands of Sikhs, whether or not they had any militant ties, were disappeared and murdered in extrajudicial killings over the span of the operation.

With rampant abuse of civilians, many Sikhs felt that the only way to deal with a government that acted above the law was through armed resistance. Babla's neighbour Pappu volunteered by storing a cache of weapons at his farm. The Punjab police had caught wind of an inventory of AK-47s somewhere in the area. Officers grabbed young Sikh men off the streets and tortured them for forced confessions, or for more information. Under duress, one tortured citizen gave up Pappu's name. Police surrounded both Pappu and Babla's homes and forced their way in.

"They found my mom first," Iqbal Kaur explained to me. She is Babla's sister and also my mother-in-law. "My mom had shoulder surgery around that time so she couldn't move her arms a lot. She still tried fighting back against the officers, but her punches couldn't stop them."

Nuvi and I sat on a white loveseat in her parents' living room. Nuvi's mother Iqbal and father Jagjit were on a matching sofa to our left. An oval-shaped glass coffee table supported by dark brown wood and a metal support frame sat in the middle of the room. A television propped in the corner across from us aired a Punjabi news program at a volume too low to hear.

"The officers held my mom and said they wouldn't hurt Babla if he gave himself up," Iqbal explained. She had her hair pulled back in a bun and her feet up on the couch, tired from her day spent working as a forklift driver at a warehouse in Mississauga. "The police lied though. They beat my brother up right in front of my mom. They took him away. Nobody saw him for weeks after that."

Jagjit turned away from the conversation and faced the TV.

"What did the police do to him?" I asked.

"Nobody knows," Nuvi said, shaking her head. "Mamma Ji doesn't like to talk about it."

The torture methods employed by the Punjab police were brutal. In some cases, electric shocks were applied to the nipples or testicles. Others had their legs pulled apart in opposite directions, causing severe damage to the hips, groin and pelvis. Some had their tailbone or feet struck repeatedly with a baton, causing bruising and swelling to the point the detainee could no longer sit or stand. The exact techniques applied to Babla are unknown—to this day, he refuses to talk to anyone about the time he spent as a captive. Though he chooses not to speak of his pain, his appearance reminds others of what he went through: Babla's legs and feet are heavily scarred, and he walks slowly and with a limp.

After being bloodied and broken down for several weeks, the police felt that Babla had no information they deemed useful and decided to let him go. Sometimes the release of a prisoner was a sign of false hope, letting the torture victim believe they were free, only to then be shot by police as they fled. These were known as 'fake encounters,' where police who murdered detainees would falsely claim that the killing was an act of self defence. Between 1984 and 1995, over 25 000 Sikhs were killed or disappeared by police in Punjab through fake encounters and extrajudicial killings. Babla was fortunate enough to be released without also being hunted down. His friends weren't as lucky.

"It was a bad time," Jagjit said. At over six feet tall and 200 pounds, my father-in-law had an intimidating presence, but he was gentle and jovial. Grey hair peppered his temples and beard stubble. His large eyes watered over and hid pain. "Five of my best friends were killed by Punjab police in the eighties, one after another," Jagjit explained. He took a sip from the glass of dark liquor cradled in his hands.

"I came to Canada in the mid-eighties to work for a few years," Iqbal said. She turned her attention to Jagjit. "Your dad kept telling you to come join me in Toronto. He was scared you would be killed by the police, like your friends were."

Jagjit shrugged. "I didn't want to leave," he said. "I didn't know anything about Canada; Punjab was home for me. After we saw what happened to Babla though, I decided I couldn't stay. I didn't do anything wrong—none of my friends did anything wrong—but the police didn't care." He took another sip and chuckled under his breath. He turned back to the television. "It was a bad time."

***

One of the reasons that I wanted to track down my family history was to understand the 'why' that caused them to leave a place and a way of living that was the only thing they had known for generations. The single but loaded answer came from Bachittar Massar Ji when he said there was no longer a future in India. For him and my father, their exodus was largely due to debt and economic factors. For my father-in-law and thousands of others, it was the trauma of state violence. In both instances, the home that they knew was changing and becoming unrecognizable. Those that could get out did what they had to do to leave. Those who couldn't leave were supported by money sent back from their siblings who had settled in the West, like Dad did for Mohinder Chacha Ji.

In learning about what had happened in Punjab in the eighties, I felt like I understood my parents more. Their lack of communication and reluctance to talk about their lives before settling in Canada made more sense to me. The past had nothing new to offer them, only pain. When they first came to Canada, their traumas were still fresh; migration didn't give them time to process any of it. Coming to a new country, they couldn't slow down to talk about the violence they had witnessed and experienced. Instead, they had to keep moving to pay the bills and feed the family. For my parents, in-laws, aunties, and uncles who had left India, their options were either to figure things out in the West despite the challenges and racism they encountered here, or go back to Punjab and deal with all the things that made home unlivable. Backed into a corner, there was no other choice but to push their traumas down beneath the surface, find a way to make things work, and let the dead rest.

It also made sense why my sister and I were raised the way we were, in a household that stressed the importance of Sikh ideals and identity. Vijay was born in 1983, and I followed in '86—right in the thick of the darkness surrounding 1984. It might have been easier, safer, for our parents to raise us in our new homeland solely as Canadians to shield us from the same discrimination they had faced here, but my family chose not to hide who we were. We were raised as Sikhs at a time when Sikhs were being targeted. Our upbringing, our being, was an act of resistance.

NOW $\frac{\text{CH}}{20}$

"Life is long but it feels so short," Dad said.

It was February 16, 2018, the morning of his last day on the job. We were both in the kitchen. He sat at the dinner table drinking cha. He had a small, white plate with scattered almonds and cashews in front of him, and his back to the sunshine beaming in through the sliding door. I stood by the sink on the other side of the kitchen and sliced fruits for a smoothie I was preparing for Mom.

"I arrived in Canada in 1982," Dad continued. "My first day was February 14. I was without a job for the first four weeks I was here, but other than that, I've been working continuously for that whole time."

It felt like Dad was eulogizing himself. He measured his worth through his service and his ability to provide—for his parents, his siblings, his wife, and his children. Dad stayed in the furniture industry for nearly the entirety of his life in Canada. He could talk endlessly about the specifics of different types of fabric, foam, and cushions; for someone who was born in a house made of mud and still slept on a thin mattress rolled out on the floor, he knew a lot about items of leisure that he himself didn't ever use. He built his life with his hands as best he could. He utilized each nail, screw, and staple to piece together a foundation that elevated himself and the family up from that entry-level position on the loading dock, to eventually becoming manager of production and part-owner of a furniture company for the final few years of his working life.

Internally, the family questioned how my father would adapt to retired life. It seemed like the older he got, the more he worked. When he became part-owner, it was common for him to log twelve-hour days during the week and still work on Saturdays when the factory was closed. He would regularly take me along with him on weekends to help clean the factory or move around heavy furniture frames and machinery that he couldn't haul on his own. We'd be the only two people in the entire building; under the dust and dim lighting that fell over us, I struggled to understand how he kept going. Even his days off were spent working on different projects around the house. I felt like I couldn't take a nap on a lazy afternoon or watch TV if Dad was home because I didn't feel I deserved to relax if he didn't allow himself the same luxury. Hustle was in his blood—to be quiet, put his head down, and get the work done, no matter what; his survival was dependent on that mindset for so long. Dad had the self-awareness to acknowledge that sitting still in retirement would be a challenge for him.

"Did I ever tell you about Waris Shah?" Dad asked me, referring to the 18th century Punjabi poet. I didn't respond. I knew he wasn't really asking me a question anyway; my answer had no bearing on what he would say next and where his train of thought was moving. "Waris Shah said that even if a person is broken down and cut into pieces, they can still be unwilling to abandon their ways. Someone's habits can only be changed when they are replaced with something else."

When I was younger, my father would often tell me about his dream to leave Canada after retirement. He would paint a romanticized image of retreating to a cave, or anywhere peaceful and uninhabited, to dedicate his time to spirituality and meditation. The paat room at home was his attempt at creating the monastic refuge he wanted for himself.

"Of all the places I've been in the world, I've never been to Bhutan," Dad said. He finished the last sip of his tea and set the cup back down on the table. "I went to Afghanistan and Nepal and saw the mountains, but Bhutan is supposed to be even more beautiful than that. I think that would be best. Up on a mountain somewhere, by myself. No worries. These days, I can make $80 in two hours. That used to be a month's salary for me." His thoughts were becoming disjointed, jumping from point to point like he was breaking himself down and tip-toeing over the scattered pieces; each shard was a different regret. "I felt like I could have done more for you, for your sister."

"What do you mean?" I asked.

I knew that he and Mom did all they possibly could for the family. There weren't any more hours in the day that they could have filled with more labour. We lived a steady middle-class life. We weren't the most well-off, but we always had enough. As a kid, we lived in a house in the suburbs: soccer practice, swimming lessons, street hockey, and a basketball hoop in the driveway. In high school, my biggest concern was getting good grades so I could go to university. From a financial standpoint, life was mostly stable for me; I didn't have to leave home to find opportunity the way my parents did. More than anything, they gave me the freedom to choose: what I wanted to study, what job I wanted to work, and to speak up without fearing state suppression or violence. For someone who spent so much time focused on spirituality, I wished Dad would see that success could be measured in more ways than just money.

"I mean wealth," Dad said. "Real wealth for your kids and their kids. I wasn't able to give that to you." Dad moved his eyes from mine and looked down at the marble tabletop. "Maybe I should have stayed in school when I got here or done a different job. Day by day, it's getting harder for your generation to afford the basic cost of living." He tucked his steel thermos into his lunch bag and left the house for his last shift.

***

After settling in Canada in 1982, Dad always planned to sponsor his parents and siblings from Nawan Pind to join him in the West. Dhadhi Ji, Dhadha Ji and Kuldip Bhua Ji first arrived in Canada around the time I was born. Their first pictures here were my first pictures after coming home from the hospital; we were all celebrating new beginnings at the time.

Kuldip Bhua Ji was the cool auntie in my family. As the youngest of Dad's siblings, she was just a teenager when she came to Canada. I remember being in junior kindergarten and flipping through her high school yearbook when she attended Westwood Secondary School in Malton. In her graduation picture, she was cloaked in a silky, navy blue robe and had her hair pulled back into two braids. She held her diploma in one hand and a bouquet of red roses in the other.

Bhua Ji didn't really know Dad very well growing up. They were seventeen years apart in age. She was a toddler and too young to remember him when he had moved from Nawan Pind to Dhilwan to go to college. She was just starting school when Dad left for Europe the first time in 1975. He was in and out of her life for the next five years, hopping back and forth between Punjab and wherever the waters took him. By 1982, Dad was in Canada. When he and Bhua Ji were reunited in Malton in the late eighties, when he was thirty-three and she was sixteen, that was really the first opportunity they had to spend consistent time with each other and build a relationship.

After sponsoring Dhadha Ji, Dhadhi Ji, and Kuldip Bhua Ji, Dad sponsored Sardara Chacha Ji in 1992. Understanding and navigating Canadian immigration laws was a challenge. As a married man who was of legal age, the laws at the time considered Mohinder Chacha Ji to be ineligible for sponsorship. Dad carried the guilt of feeling that he had left Mohinder behind.

Growing up, I always wondered why we didn't have more pictures in Canada of what my parents' life was like in Punjab. Aside from their wedding album and Dad's passports, I hadn't seen many other pictures of Mom, Dad, or their siblings from the time before they settled in the West. In my entire life, I had only ever seen two photos of Dad from his years spent as a sailor: one of him and Raj in the quarters of their ship sporting mustaches and long hair that could only be fashionable at the height of the disco era, and another of them at a bar in Europe somewhere. I just attributed the lack of photos to their inability to afford a camera back in the sixties and seventies. However, I learned from my cousin—Mohinder Chacha Ji's daughter, Raman—that older pictures of the family do exist, and they're kept in Nawan Pind.

When Raman was heading from Toronto to Punjab in 2018 to visit her parents in the village, I asked her if she could bring some pictures back to Canada when she returned. Raman told me she couldn't do that; those pictures would never leave Nawan Pind. Separated from his siblings, those photographs would remain safely with Mohinder Chacha Ji as a way for him to stay close to his family that had left Punjab.

***

In Dad's first few official days of retirement, he tried his best to live his version of the mountain life he wanted for himself. He took more time to meditate and read, but found that this wasn't as fulfilling as he dreamt it would be. While taking time to pray, study, and reflect were important parts of his daily routine, he needed more stimulation to keep his mind and hands busy in the absence of more tangible work to do.

Before Mom got sick, she and Dad would often go on walks together in the summers. Since retiring though, Dad started to take walks alone every morning despite it being February and the coldest part of winter. While at home with Mom, Dad prepared her meals, dressed her wounds, and massaged her aching muscles, but that would still only total a few hours of the day. Now that he finally had a chance to slow down, he didn't know how to; he felt like he still had more to give.

Dad took Mom to meet with Dr. Higgins at Sunnybrook Hospital in April 2018. We had waited for this appointment ever since Mom's surgery the previous September. Finally making it to this point, we felt as if we were marathon runners with deflated lungs, swollen knees, splinting shins, and bloody feet trying our best to drag our hobbling bodies over the finish line. It had been a long and difficult winter for all of us; we prayed that spring would offer us renewal. Dr. Higgins told Mom she wouldn't need another round of chemotherapy or radiation, and that he would continue to monitor her every few weeks. Despite the good news of Mom's cancer status, it didn't bring about the desired relief for any of us. As much as we had hoped for a positive outcome at this appointment, Mom's day to day existence was still a struggle—to eat, to breathe, to walk, to sleep, to speak. She still lived in constant pain. This existence was the new reality that cancer had set for us and there was no going back from it.

***

"Come, follow me." Dad said. It was October 2018. He had just turned sixty-five. "I'll show you around."

Nuvi and I walked behind him. Our steps left footprints in the dusty concrete floor. The lights overhead bathed the bricks and drywall with a grimy shade of yellow. Dad showed us around the warehouse space in Toronto that he was going to lease. In the months after Mom's meeting with Dr. Higgins, Dad had made plans to start his own furniture company. He even had a name for the business—Studio 289 Furniture—titled after the area code that surrounded Toronto. He said he was starting this business to give something to me and Vijay, and that if it was profitable, it could be something we passed down to future generations. Maybe that really was Dad's motivation, but it felt like this business was more for himself. Waris Shah was right: broken down and removed of the thing that gave him purpose, Dad couldn't find anything to replace his old habits.

"I'm thinking we could set up the sewing machines here," Dad said while pointing to an empty space on the floor to his right. He took a few more steps and pointed to another empty space on his left. "And I could set up my cutting tables and shelves for my rolls of fabric here."

Dad's voice echoed off the beams in the high ceiling. He walked with an excitement in his step. Nuvi and I had to be quick to keep up. Dad waved an arm at where the showroom would go and what kind of pieces he would display there. He saw mirages in the blank slate that was the empty warehouse, and he animated life wherever he pointed his hands like it was his super power. If we looked close enough, we could see his visions too.

I understood why Dad wanted to start this new business now at a point in his life when most people his age would be looking forward to resting. Since he was a child, he didn't have a say in what he wanted for himself. On the farm, he had to do as his father told him. On the ships, he was under the orders of the captain. With Custom Upholstery, he listened to his uncles to guide the direction of the business. Even as part-owner of a company before he retired, Dad had the fewest shares and the smallest slice of the pie. This new venture was something that Dad was creating from the bottom-up. For the first time in his life, he was doing something entirely for himself. There was no other time to do it but now.

**

By 2019, Mom's pain only got worse. Beginning in February, her left jaw bone, which had absorbed the brunt of the radiation when she was still in treatment, got infected several times. The pain kept Mom awake at night; she had to be careful of how she lay down as the wrong position would cause her jaw to move. The pain of that movement broke Mom down to tears every time. Dad took her to the ER to get checked out on a few occasions, but none of the doctors' recommendations seemed to help. On August 20, 2019, Mom was scheduled to meet with Dr. Higgins. Dad asked that I attend the appointment with them so that nothing the doctor said would get lost in translation.

"How's the pain been?" Dr. Higgins asked. He took a seat in a stool with metal legs and rubber wheels and sat in front of Mom. I sat in a chair to Mom's left. Dr. Higgins wore seafoam green scrubs under a white lab coat, and had a black surgical headlamp strapped to his forehead. A younger male doctor stood next to him clad in identical scrubs.

"Lots of pain in my jaw," Mom described. "Sometimes it's so bad that I can't speak." The younger doctor scribbled notes on his clipboard.

"I looked at the results of your latest bloodwork and CT scan," Dr. Higgins said. "The good news is that the cancer isn't back. The complication though is that the radiation killed the bone in your jaw. That's what has been causing your recent pain. The muscles, tissues, and blood vessels in your neck are dead too."

I thought of how a cruel an irony it was that the side effects of the cure were as damaging as the symptoms of the sickness.

Dr. Higgins pulled a latex glove from his chest pocket and snapped it over his hand. He ran his fingers over the discoloured skin on Mom's left shoulder. "Your neck is like hollow wood at this point," he said, "and the skin is paper thin."

"What can we do?" Dad asked. He stood in the far corner of the room. He wanted me to take the seat next to Mom so I could be closer to the doctor and ask the medical questions that Dad felt he didn't have the vocabulary for.

Dr. Higgins turned in his stool to face Dad. "Unfortunately, this pain is the cost of survivorship. Her disease was so advanced and aggressive. To be honest, I'm surprised she's survived as long as she has. We see this kind of thing with radiation where the treatment can kill the cancer but it also kills the bone. We'll be looking at options to surgically remove the bone, maybe replace it with a metal plate of some sort. Give us some time to figure things out and we'll get her into surgery as soon as possible. We'll call you to schedule a follow-up appointment to do some bloodwork."

Dr. Higgins rose from his seat and shook each of our hands. There wasn't much that needed to be translated. We all understood what the doctor meant—more appointments, more living with the unknown, more pain.

Still, regardless of what Mom had faced over the past two years, she physically and mentally didn't give in to her illness. The fact that the doctor didn't expect her to make it this far was a testament to her strength. The proof of her resilience was in her scars. From that day forward, Mom helped me see things in a different way: when there's no going back to the way things used to be, we must do the best we can with what we have now.

***

As the saying goes, if we don't know where we're coming from, we won't know where we're going. The migratory generation in my family knew where they came from, but didn't know where they were going, or if what they found at their destination would match what they were told would be there. In my generation, the reality was the opposite. As part of the first generation of my family born outside of Punjab, my cousins and I were removed in time and space from what our elders historically referred to as home. Through the sacrifices of our parents, we had the privilege to decide where we wanted to go and what we wanted to do, but lacked the knowledge of where we came from.

To understand my future and my present, I had to look to the past. When Nani Ji and Gurmukh Thaya Ji died and Mom got sick all within the span of five months, I tried to unearth a lineage that I was disconnected from and felt I was getting farther away from as each elder left this plane of existence. In sitting down and speaking with some of my elders who were still alive, I learned of stories that varied in intensity and significance, from the traumatic to the mundane, but they all helped paint a broader picture of lives lived.

There were many lessons I soaked in along the way. From my father's years farming, I learned the importance of patience, and to honour everything the earth gives us. From his faith, I learned how to be grateful for all things. From his time crossing borders, I learned resourcefulness, and that sometimes it's better to take the long way to get to where you're trying to go. I also learned how home can change, and how leaving a situation can sometimes become the only logical choice. From Dad's years sailing, I learned that life is much like water—sometimes it flows and sometimes it crashes. Sometimes we let the waves carry us, and other times we need to swim against the current for survival. While chasing old ghosts though, I was missing out on the larger lessons that the universe was trying to teach all of us.

In caring for Mom after her surgery throughout the winter of 2017, we hung our hopes on the calendar and prayed for the clarity of spring when the snow would melt away, new life would blossom, and Mom would meet with Dr. Higgins again. Within that longing though, we lost sight of what we had in front of us. Getting to April wasn't promised; all we had was now. All that we could do to comfort each other, to give love to each other, to help one another heal, and to build something, had to be done in the now. There wasn't a chance we would get to do those things in the future because, through illness and through death and through migration, we didn't know if that future would ever come. My parents taught me how to honour the present and to value the importance of now. Now is an opportunity. Now is all we have.

My parents also taught me about hope. At our darkest times, hope can ring hollow if not also accompanied by action. Hope shouldn't just be a wish for things to get better. Hope is more than thinking positively. From my grandfather finding ways to provide for the family during the floods, to my father leaving home and risking his freedom and safety around the globe to break the cycle of poverty, to the way we cared for my mother in her most vulnerable moments—for hope to become anything other than false and intangible sentiment, it cannot be passive. Hope is the way we fight for ourselves. What we do matters, and what we do now is vital. Hope is an action.

Notes

1   **In the song "A Story No One Told," rapper Shad tells the tale**
www.genius.com/Shad-a-story-no-one-told-lyrics

1   **James Baldwin said that history does not exist in the past**
Arica Coleman, "James Baldwin Documentary 'I Am Not Your Negro'
Is the Product of a Specific Moment in History," Time, February 24,
2017, www.time.com/4680673/james-baldwin-documentary-history

4   **Growing up in Derby as a teenager in the late sixties**
Shannyn Quinn, "Tributes paid as founder of Derby's Sohal Food dies
aged 65," Derby Telegraph, July 12, 2017, www.derbytelegraph.co.uk/
news/derby-news/tributed-paid-founder-derbys-sohal-190562

45   **The Indian government introduced a middleman system**
Debiprasad Nayak, "Farmers Struggle to Escape Middlemen,"
The Wall Street Journal, February 26, 2014, https://blogs.wsj.com/
indiarealtime/2014/02/26/farmers-struggle-to-escape-middlemen

48   **The Green Revolution marked a change in farming practices**
Nelson, A., et al. (2019). The impact of the Green Revolution on
indigenous crops of India. *Journal of Ethnic Foods, 6*(8),
https://doi.org/10.1186/s42779-019-0011-9.

48   **The state of Bihar—another region in India that, much like**
Jean Dreze, *The Political Economy of Hunger Volume 2: Famine
Prevention* (New York: Oxford University Press, 1990), p. 59.

50   **Data from Punjab Agricultural University shows that at least**
Kanwalroop Kaur, "A pattern of farmer suicides in Punjab:
Unearthing the Green Revolution," KALW, December 4, 2018, https://
www.kalw.org/post/pattern-farmer-suicides-punjab-unearthing-
green-revolution#stream/0

50   **Critics of The Green Revolution have stated that in the**
Daniel Zwerdling, "In Punjab, Crowding Onto The Cancer Train,"
NPR, May 11, 2009, https://www.npr.org/templates/story/
story.php?storyId=103569390

52   **Military tensions between India and Pakistan had ramped up**
Asad Hashim, "Timeline: India-Pakistan Relations,"
Al Jazeera, March 1, 2019, www.aljazeera.com/indepth/spotlight/
kashmirtheforgottenconflict/2011/06/2011615113058224115.html

61   **In 1970, there were 31 000 applications submitted by people**
Canadian Council for Refugees, "A hundred years of immigration to
Canada 1900-1999," https://ccrweb.ca/en/hundred-years-
immigration-canada-part-2

66   **Justin Trudeau famously called diversity a source of strength**
Jake Horowitz, "How Canadian Prime Minister Justin Trudeau
Won Over Millenials At Davos," Mic, January 25, 2016, www.
mic.com/articles/133321/can-you-guess-which-world-leader-won-
over-millennials-at-davos

66   **Canadian settlers also enslaved Black and Indigenous people**
Kyle Brown, "Canada's slavery secret: The whitewashing of 200 years
of enslavement," CBC, February 18, 2019, www.cbc.ca/radio/ideas/
canada-s-slavery-secret-the-whitewashing-of-200-years-of-
enslavement-1.4726313

66   **In 2016, a coroner's inquest into the fatal police shooting**
Wendy Gillis, "Peel cop sought to card Jermaine Carby before slaying,
inquest hears," The Toronto StarMay 12, 2016, www.thestar.com/
news/crime/2016/05/12/peel-cop-sought-to-card-jermaine-
carby-before-slaying-inquest-hears.html

67   **Also in 2016, an Indigenous man named Colten Boushie was shot**
Andray Domise, "What the tragedy of Colten Boushie says about
racism in Canada," Maclean's, August 25, 2016, www.macleans.ca/
news/canada/the-tragedy-of-colten-boushie-racism-canada/

76   **Jawaharlal Nehru believed that political and economic**
      "Industrialization in India after Independence," Current Affairs India,
      August, 1, 2013, www.currentaffairsindia.info/2013/08/
      industrialization-in-india-after-independence.html

82   **the Organization of Arab Petroleum Exporting Countries instated**
      Tomas Hirst, "All of Greece's problems can be traced back to the
      1970s," The Journal.ie, March 22, 2015, www.thejournal.ie/
      greece-problems-1970s-explainer-1994793-Mar2015/

115   **The first 5000 Indian settlers arrived in British Columbia**
      Nancy Demwell, "North Delta History: South Asian settlement
      throughout the 20th century," Surrey Now-Leader, June 10, 2018,
      www.surreynowleader.com/community/north-delta-history-south-
      asian-settlement-throughout-the-20th-century/#

115   **In 1885, the Canadian government instituted a Chinese Head Tax**
      Matthew McRae, "The Chinese Head Tax and the Chinese Exclusion
      Act," Canadian Museum for Human Rights, https://humanrights.ca/
      story/the-chinese-head-tax-and-the-chinese-exclusion-act

115   **In 1903, this tax was increased to $500 as a way to deter further**
      Sarjeet Singh Jagpal, *Becoming Canadians: Pioneer Sikhs in Their
      Own Words* (Vancouver: Harbour Publishing, 1994), p. 22.

116   **H.H. Stevens, an alderman for the city of Vancouver, stated that**
      Sarjeet Singh Jagpal, Becoming Canadians: Pioneer Sikhs in Their
      Own Words (Vancouver: Harbour Publishing, 1994), p. 26.

117   **One notable example was that of Ajit Kaur, the daughter of farm**
      Sarjeet Singh Jagpal, Becoming Canadians: Pioneer Sikhs in Their
      Own Words (Vancouver: Harbour Publishing, 1994), p. 138.

117   **Several neighbourhoods in Brampton were covered in flyers**
      "Brampton residents outraged by anti-immigration flyers," CTV News
      Toronto, April 25, 2014, https://toronto.ctvnews.ca/brampton-
      residents-outraged-by-anti-immigration-flyers-1.1792719

117   **A white woman stormed the stage at one of Jagmeet's town hall**
Linda Givetash, "Heckler at Jagmeet Singh event an example of
racism in Canada, prof says," CTV News, September 9, 2017, www.
ctvnews.ca/politics/heckler-at-jagmeet-singh-event-an-example-of-
racism-in-canada-prof-says-1.3582794

144   **Thousands of Sikh men throughout the seventies had been**
Knut Jacobsen & Kristina Myrvold, *Sikhs in Europe: Migration,
Identities, and Representations* (Surrey: Ashgate Publishing Limited,
2011), p. 167

144   **In 1971, Indira Gandhi had defeated Raj Narain to become India's**
Sikh Research Institiute, "The Emergency & The Sikhs," https://
www.sikhri.org/the_emergency_the_sikhs

145   **The state of emergency ended nearly two years later in March of**
Inder Malhotra, *Indira Gandhi: A Personal Political Biography*
(London: Hodder and Stoughton, 1989), p. 178

161   **writer and activist WEB DuBois coined the term 'double**
W.E. Bughardt Du Bois, "Strivings of the Negro People," The Atlantic,
August 1897, https://www.theatlantic.com/magazine/
archive/1897/08/strivings-of-the-negro-people/305446/

161   **On the track "Man By Choice," Toronto rap legend Kardinal**
https://genius.com/Kardinal-offishall-man-by-choice-lyrics

162   **Even Sikhs who had achieved mainstream success and fame**
Christine Hauser, "Turban-Wearing Sikh American Actor Is Barred
from AeroMexico," The New York Times, February 8, 2016, https://
www.nytimes.com/2016/02/09/world/turban-wearing-american-
actor-is-barred-from-aeromexico-flight.html

180   **I read about how mobs armed with iron rods and kerosene**
Simran Jeet Singh, "It's Time India Accept Responsibility for Its 1984
Sikh Genocide," Time, October 31, 2014, https://time.com/3545867/
india-1984-sikh-genocide-anniversary

180 **how Sikh women were gang-raped**
Amarjit Singh Walia, "I lived through the Sikh riots - and 30 years later, I'm not ready to forgive or forget," Quartz India, October 31, 2014, https://qz.com/india/289671/i-lived-through-the-sikh-riots-and-30-years-later-im-not-ready-to-forgive-or-forget

180 **how bodies were set aflame with tires around their necks**
Gurpreet Singh, "The world's silence over the 1984 Sikh massacre needs to be broken," The Georgia Straight, November 1, 2018, https://www.straight.com/news/1159501/gurpreet-singh-worlds-silence-over-1984-sikh-massacre-needs-be-broken

180 **how chemical weapons like white phosphorous were used**
Pav Singh, *1984: India's Guilty Secret* (London: Allison & Busby, Ltd., 2019), ch. 3

180 **how burnt bodies were stacked on top of each other**
Jarnail Singh, *I Accuse...The Anti-Sikh Violence of 1984,* (New Delhi: Penguin India, 2009), p. 46

180 **how historical Sikh libraries were burned to the ground**
Surjit Singh, "The Missing Chapter of 1984: Book by book, Sikh Reference Library struggles to restore glory," Hindustan Times, June 6, 2018, www.hindustantimes.com/punjab/the-missing-chapter-of-1984-book-by-book-sikh-library-struggles-to-restore-glory/story-UR8vtpo8NrjVpE8eK4agoN.html

181 **While Muslims were a minority in India, making up a quarter of**
Ishtiaq Ahmed, "The Punjab Bloodied, Partitioned and Cleansed," Fair Observer, January 31, 2013, https://www.fairobserver.com/region/central_south_asia/punjab-bloodied-partitioned-and-cleansed

181 **a movement calling for an independent Muslim nation to be**
Monica Sarkar, "Faith, fury and fear: The story behind one of history's greatest mass migrations," CNN, August 15, 2018, https://www.cnn.com/2017/08/08/asia/india-pakistan-independence-timeline/index.html

181 **Though Sikhs were also a minority in India who made up only**
Kristin Bakke, *Decenralization and Intrastate Struggles: Chechnya, Punjab, and Quebec* (New York: Cambridge University Press, 2015), p. 134

181 **As India approached independence, Indian Prime Minister**
Aman Sidhu, *Debt and Death in Rural India: The Punjab Story* (New Delhi: Sage Publications, 2011), ch. 6

181 **After two centuries of colonial rule, the last viceroy of British**
Adil Najam, "How a British royal's monuental errors made India's partition more painful," The Conversation, August 15, 2017, https://theconversation.com/how-a-british-royals-monumental-errors-made-indias-partition-more-painful-81657

182 **Punjab's governor Chandu Lal Trivedi issued a statement that**
Gurmit Singh, *History of Sikh Struggles, Vol. 1, 1946-1966* (New Delhi: Atlantic Publishers & Distributors, 1992), p. 51

182 **Many of the existing state borders in India were relics that**
Harbans Singh, *The Encyclopaedia of Sikhism* (Delhi: Punjabi University, 1997), p. 391

182 **Nehru's decision to change borders on linguistic grounds was**
Pranay Gupte, *Mother India: A Political Biography of Indira Gandhi* (New Delhi: Penguin Books, 2009), p. 301

182 **To spite the ban, over 10 000 Sikhs intentionally courted arrest**
Sadhna Sharma, *State Politics in India* (New Delhi: Mittal Publications, 1995), p. 324

183 **In a tactic designed to snuff out the movement, police launched**
Ajit Sarhadi, *Punjabi Suba: The Story of Struggle* (Delhi: U.C. Kapur & Sons, 1970), p. 248

183 **Of the fourteen official languages recognized in India's**
Kristin Bakke, *Decenralization and Intrastate Struggles: Chechnya, Punjab, and Quebec* (New York: Cambridge University Press, 2015), p. 140

183   **The identity of Sikhs was closely tied to the Punjabi language**
Kristin Bakke, *Decenralization and Intrastate Struggles: Chechnya, Punjab, and Quebec* (New York: Cambridge University Press, 2015), p. 138

183   **Under the Punjab Reorganization Act in 1966, Punjab's borders**
Kristin Bakke, *Decenralization and Intrastate Struggles: Chechnya, Punjab, and Quebec* (New York: Cambridge University Press, 2015), p. 141

183   **Farming was the lifeblood of Punjab's economy and accounted**
Sadhna Sharma, *State Politics in India* (New Delhi: Mittal Publications, 1995), p. 310

183   **Under international law, and as outlined in India's constitution**
Biplab Tripathy, *Water Crisis in India* (Bilaspur: Evincepub Publishing, 2019), p. 29

183   **With the introduction of The Green Revolution and the demands**
"Why Punjab has a water crisis, and what now," The Punjabi Tribune, July 1, 2019, www.tribuneindia.com/news/archive/features/why-punjab-has-a-water-crisis-and-what-now-795509

184   **To express their discontent with how Sikhs were treated along**
J.C. Aggarwal, *Modern History of Punjab: A Look Back Into Ancient Peaceful Punjab Focusing Confrontation and Failures Leading to Present Punjab Problem and a Peep Ahead* (New Delhi: Concept Publishing Company, 1992), p. 92

184   **By putting the country in a state of emergency in June 1975**
Aman Sidhu, *Debt and Death in Rural India: The Punjab Story* (New Delhi: Sage Publications, 2011), ch. 6

189   **However, reports indicate that anywhere from 1000 to 5000**
Inderjit Jaijee, *Politics of Genocide: Punjab, 1984-1994* (Delhi: Ajanta Publications, 1995), p. 98.

189   **Anti-Sikh violence facilitated by Gandhi's Congress Party**
Suridhi Sharma, "The horrors of 1984", February 11, 2018, Deccan
Chronicle, https://www.deccanchronicle.com/sunday-chronicle/
shelf-life/110218/the-horrors-of-1984.html

189   **Human rights groups place the death toll of Sikhs in Delhi after**
Inderjit Jaijee, *Politics of Genocide: Punjab, 1984-1994* (Delhi: Ajanta
Publications, 1995), p. 150.

189   **Following Operation Blue Star, the Indian government**
Harnik Deol, *Religion and Nationalism in India: The Case of the
Punjab* (London:Taylor & Francis, 2000), p. 108

190   **The torture methods employed by the Punjab police were brutal**
Laws, A. & Iacopino, V. (2002), Police Torture in Punjab, India: An
Extended Survey. *Health and Human Rights*, *6*(1), https://cdn1.sph.
harvard.edu/wp-content/uploads/sites/2469/2013/07/12-Laws.pdf

191   **Between 1984 and 1995, over 25 000 Sikhs were killed by**
Mallika Kaur, "Punjab: Murders Without Murderers," December 15,
2017, The Diplomat, https://thediplomat.com/2017/12/
punjab-murders-without-murderers/

Acknowledgements

Thanks to the elders who sat down with me and shared their life stories: Dad, Mom, Bachittar Massar Ji, Kulwinder Massi Ji, Kuldip Bhua Ji, Harbhajan Dhillon, Harjit Mama Ji, Nirmal Mami Ji, Iqbal Kaur, and Jagjit Singh. None of this would be possible with you. To Nuvi—thank you for being everything you are. To the cousins who dug through their old family photo albums when I called you with a question—thanks for putting up with me.

Thanks to my mentors who may or may not have been aware that they were my teachers: Marina Nemat, Chris Cameron, Jasmin Kaur, Humble the Poet, Rupi Kaur, my classmates at the University of Toronto, and the SAN family.

Eternal gratitude to the doctors and nurses at Sunnybrook for their continued care of my mother.

Thanks to everyone who made music with me and shared their incredible talents to help create the soundtrack to this book: EMPWER, Keerat Kaur, B Magic, Selena Dhillon, Jasmin, Vaz, Daysdeaf, Satnam Singh Chatha, Inaam, and Harpreet Singh. I would like to acknowledge the generous support of the Ontario Arts Council in funding the creation and recording of this project.

Finally, thank you for reading this book! This is just one story. I hope you use this to discover your histories and share your stories with the world.

About the Author

Amrit Singh is an author, rapper, spoken word artist, and community organizer from Brampton, Ontario. Some of his verses discussing themes of migration, identity, and belonging have been published in the academic journal *Sikh Formations*, and in the book *The Precarious Diasporas of Sikh and Ahmadiyya Generations: Violence, Memory, and Agency*. Amrit studied psychology and neuroscience at McMaster University, and went on to complete his masters in cognitive psychology at York University. He has facilitated Hip-Hop & Mental Health workshops in schools and community spaces in Canada, the United States, and the United Kingdom.

Best known as the rapper Noyz, Amrit has performed across North America and the UK, and has graced stages at SXSW and the Toronto International Film Festival. Amrit is also the co-host of *The Immigrant Hustle*, a podcast where he and B Magic interview individuals to discuss their stories as immigrants and children of immigrants. Through this work, Amrit aims to create a space where readers and listeners feel seen and connected with humanity.

Keep Moving On is Amrit's first book. Follow him on all social media platforms @noyzhiphop, or visit his website www.noyzhiphop.com for more information.

CPSIA information can be obtained
at www.ICGtesting.com
Printed in the USA
BVHW052337281020
592072BV00004BA/13